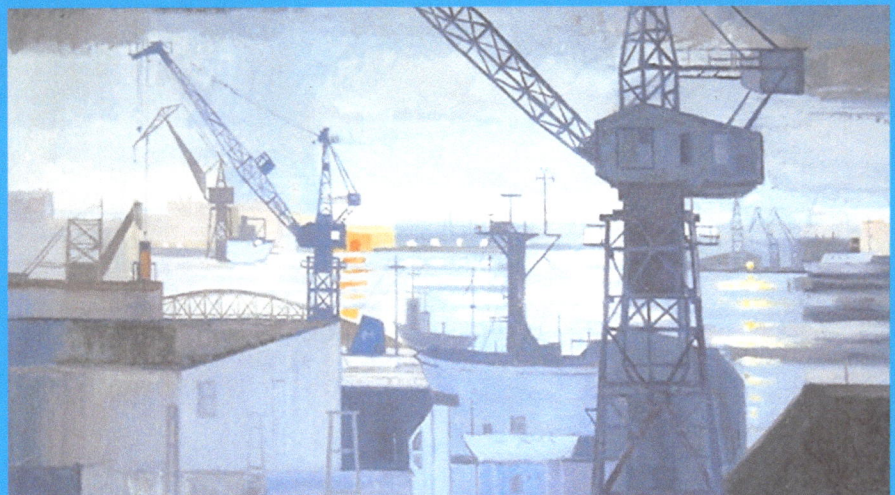

River Tyne
1974

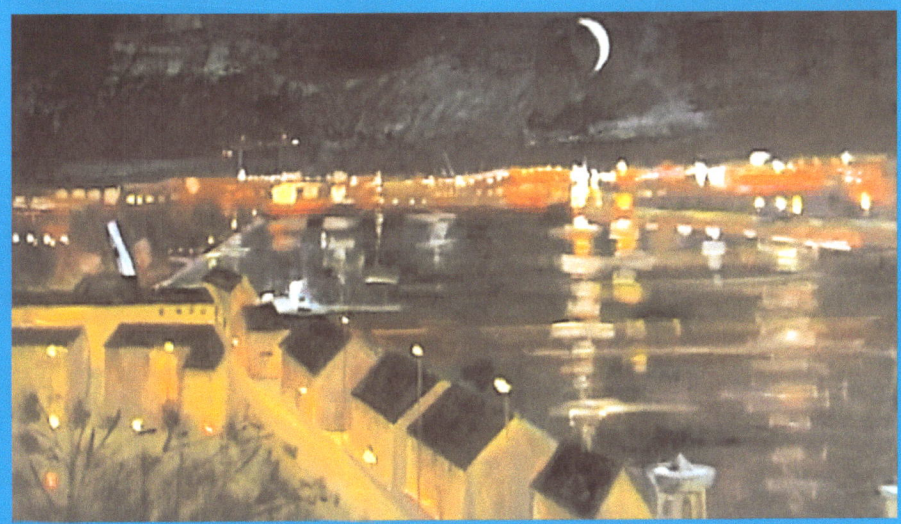

RIver Tyne
2004
from the same viewpoint

My Tyneside

A Personal Journey
by Sheila Graber

This book is dedicated to all my fellow sandancers
past, present and future.

Like *me Ma* used to say..
we are
"*aaltigither* like the folks of Shields"

All images and text created by Sheila Graber
Edited by Jane Miller

ISBN-13: 978-1480111097

Published by QuiziCat Productions

Colley's Farm
1951

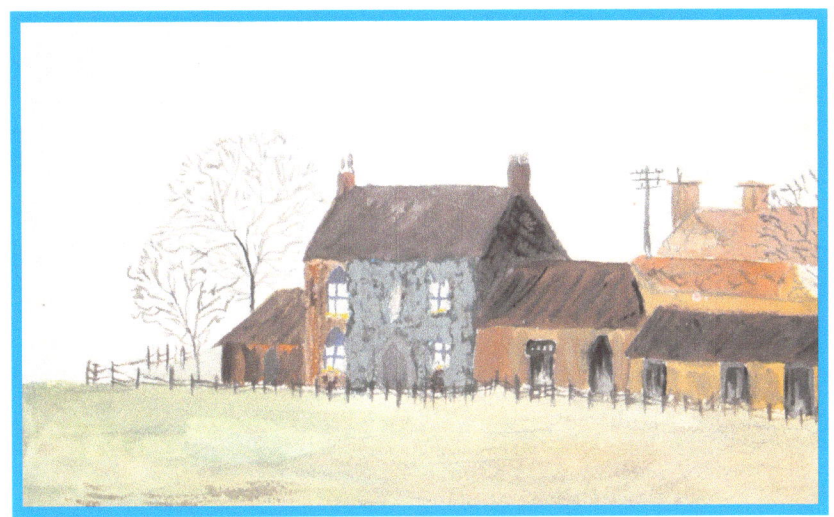

Marsden Bay
2004

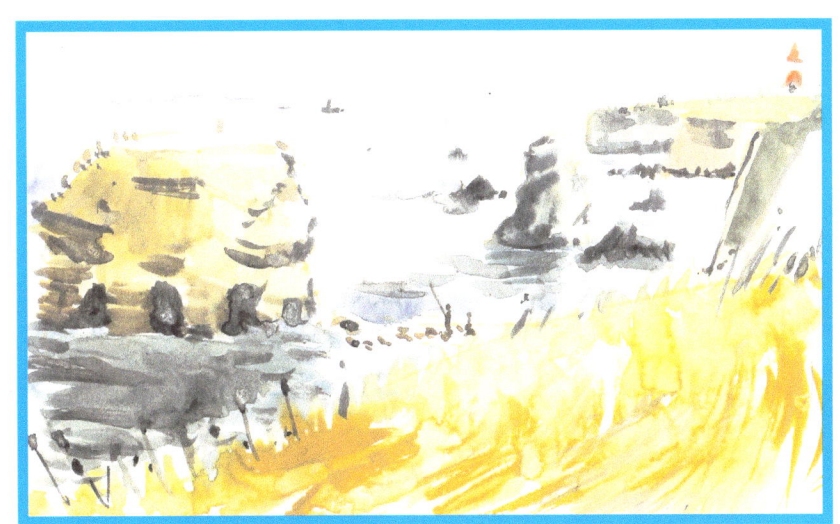

My Tyneside

A Personal Journey
by Sheila Graber
from 1951 to 2004

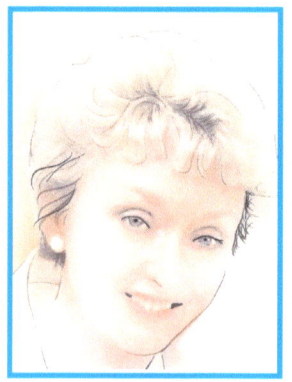

Hildred Whale
Information & Education Co-ordinator S/Tyneside Libraries (retired)

Hildred has supported my work for over 40 yrs as librarian & friend.

Sheila has always been a great champion of libraries as she understands the many strands of the activities within them and how they can help to shape and change people's lives. Her enthusiasm is what always impresses me-enthusiasm for people, for her work and for yours...whatever it is.

She is a great tonic. As a friend, she is one of those very special magical people, who can dissolve time. You may not have seen her for a while but when you do, you pickup exactly where you left off. You could have seen her yesterday!

Tyneside is home. I would never go too far away from it or for very long and coming home is one of the best feelings in the world. Coming home by road, I love it when you see the signs which say 'THE NORTH.' That thrills me, as it means I am going back to my history, heritage and home...and on the train crossing the Tyne on the railway bridge, seeing the Tyne Bridge, floodlit, again a great thrill and a wonderful warm glow which means home and safety and contentment.

They say that wherever you go in the world you will always meet a Geordie and it's remarkable how often that Geordie is a Sandancer. These Geordies are a proud people and they have a lot to be proud of, for they have always made their contribution to the nation and to the world. Great inventions, engineering, shipbuilding, huge talents in the artistic and cultural worlds and even in our own very small area we can go right back and think of Bede, the Lifeboat and of all our continuing but changing industrial skills. Geordies or Tynesiders will go on, I have no doubt, making their contribution and I am proud to be one of them.

John Lightfoot MBE - Chairman of Solar Solve Ltd

John was my first patron and has always encouraged my work.

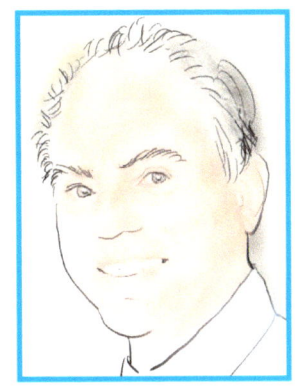

My early Tyneside was a great place to be brought up. I was lucky to live on the Marsden estate in South Shields, with the beach and acres of green belt land to play in. The freedom was taken for granted; indeed everything was taken for granted..

At the age of 18 I went off to sea to see the world and it made me appreciate the great place I call home.

In just about every port I visited they knew about Tyneside. Even today I still travel the world talking to people involved in the global marine industry and the reputation remains. Tyneside engineers are still involved in the design and construction of sophisticated vessels worldwide and South Shields Marine School is respected globally as premier marine education establishment.

I first met Sheila when she was 13 As a classmate of my sister Brenda she was visiting our house. She had gone for a walk 'over the field' to the dene, which had a few trees in it as well as loads of grass and thistles and dead man's oatmeal and blackberry bushes and stuff. I was sent to get her for tea or something (being 4 years younger and a lad you can guess where I came in hierarchy - there was nobody below me). She was sketching the trees and flowers near our house I was gobsmacked at the pencil sketch and I was fascinated by her artistic skills and have been ever since. She gave it to my Mam and it was kept for years. Sheila is a clever lass!

Marsden bay and Grotto as it was in 1940. Commissioned by John for his Mam.

5

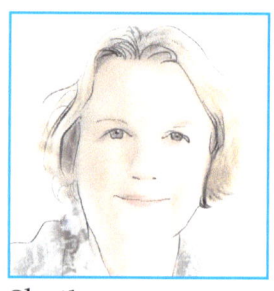

Janis Blower-
Features Writer/Cookson Country Editor
Shields Gazette
I taught Janis art, she has taught me about writing, as I have read
and enjoyed her articles over many years. We are lucky to have this
Nationally acclaimed journalist on our local paper.

Sheila gave me an appreciation of art, even though, despite her efforts , I felt I had no facility for it. But I could write. It was the only thing I was any good at, and it helped that I was blessed to have been born and brought-up in a place - the ancient headland of the Lawe in Shields - where history and stories have a habit of seeping into your consciousness almost unbidden.

And then there was being from Tyneside itself, a place that wears its heart on its sleeve, cut through with a wide and enduring river which, when you cross it - whether over one of its great bridges or on the canny Shields ferry - is like stepping over a familiar threshold.

You know you're home.

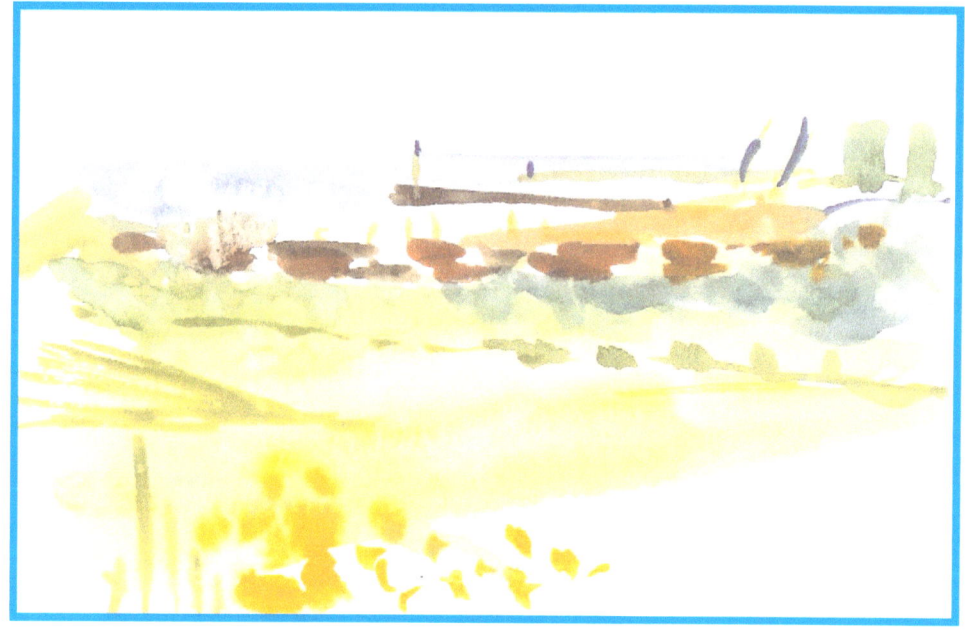

View of the Piers at the Mouth of the Tyne from Cleadon Hills, water colour 2004

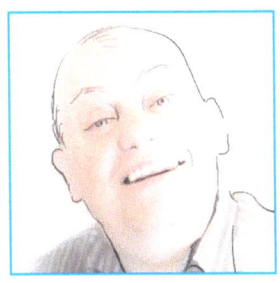

Ray Spencer MBE - Director of the Customs House S/Shields
When I first met Ray as "Tommy the Trumpeter " he suggested I might animate him. I think he's animated enough don't you?

I first became aware of Sheila's work courtesy of BBC Look North who would occasionally show award winning animations by this gifted artist. To then find out we both lived in South Shields was even more amazing, you see artists didn't come from Shields.

Pitmen, shipyard and factory workers came from Shields, not internationally acclaimed award winning animators. I later worked on a couple of projects with Sheila and Jen. Sheila was so supportive of my feeble efforts at script, that did not do justice to her brilliant animation but we laughed a lot. I should not have been surprised, as Sheila has spent her life encouraging people to feel that art is for them. Her heart is as big as our region. Like her art she is ageless, as enthusiastic and open to new ideas and technologies as she has always been. She shares her talent as generously as she shares her time, and she now shares her Tyneside with us.

I, like Sheila, love the place. I work in an arts centre that used to be a Customs House. My office overlooks a derelict shipyard where my dad worked as a caulker burner for 42 years across the rive. I see Cruise liners visiting the coaly Tyne, yes, times have changed. Fortunately, for us, who have lived through those changes, and for the generations who are yet to come, Sheila has recorded some of that heritage and shares it with us.

The North East has given me a value system. Its paternal industrialists did lots to scar its landscape but gave jobs to thousands, the land is now fighting back. I work overlooking the river, the artery to the regions beating heart. As a child the river was so loud it hurt my little boy ears. The ships were three a breast waiting to dock. The river worked to the tide, not the clock, so often men would work through the night. I remember launch days when the whole community would line the banks. They may not have worked on the ship but would know some one who did. People here worked hard in tough conditions so they loved to party. On New Years Eve the ships hooters would sound at midnight and we would go from neighbour to neighbour first footing. We seemed to like doing things together from marching and getting a "bloody" orange on Good Friday to cheering floats in the sports week parade. Or turning out in tens of thousands to look at a plate of vegetables entered in the flower show.

When you stand on Cleadon Hills you can see a lot of Tyneside and on the wind you can feel centuries of Pride in a place that made things and shared them with the world.

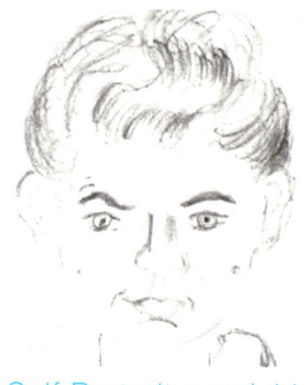

I was lucky enough to be able to mess about with paint and plasticine from an early age. None of my scribbles have survived, "thank goodness" do I hear you say? However I have still hold, by pure chance and lucky accident a collection of art work that stretches in an almost unbroken line from 1951 when I started "The Girl's High School" in South Shields to 2004 when I left to live in Ireland.

I moved away from "sandancer land" in order to collect my thoughts and my work together. This book is the result. I hope it brings back many memories for you and yours.

My formative years were spent at 3 Lavington Road. Directly opposite us was "Wood's Garden" . My Mam said she remembers Mr Wood strolling through the garden smoking his cigar after dinner. My brother Peter and I just remembered it as a great place to climb trees, when no one was looking! The last time I saw the house it was a care home.

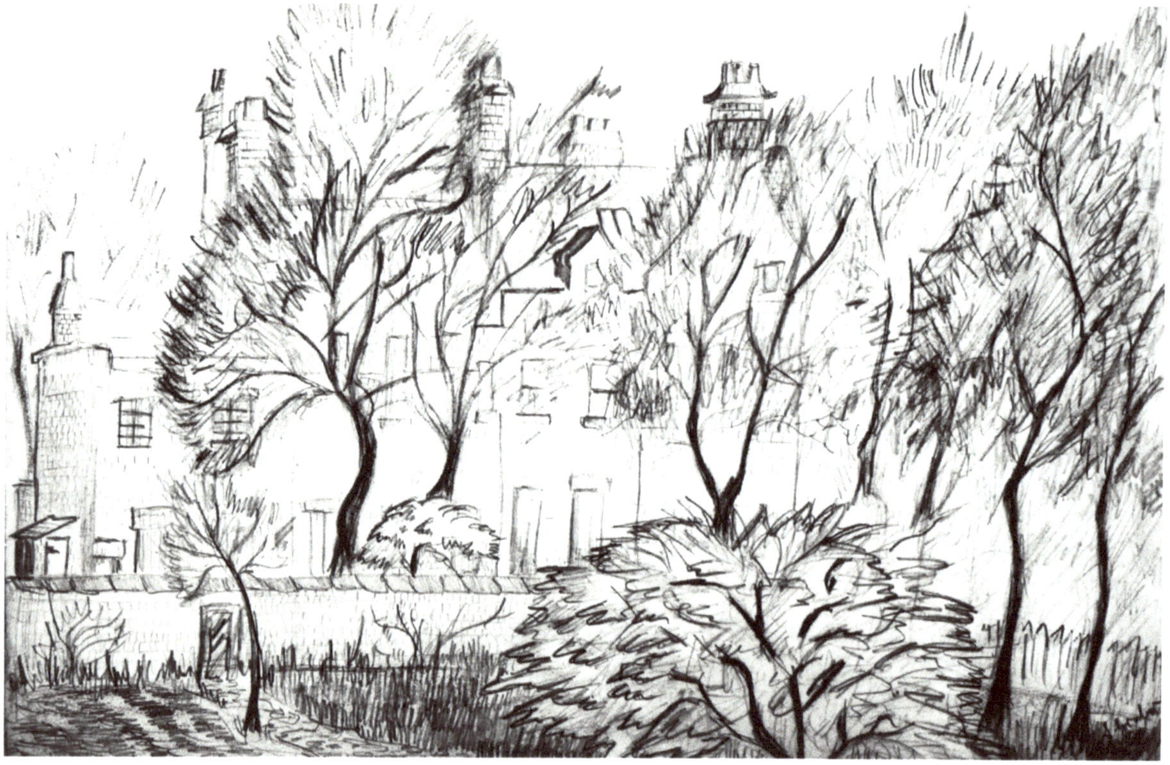

Wood's Garden 1951

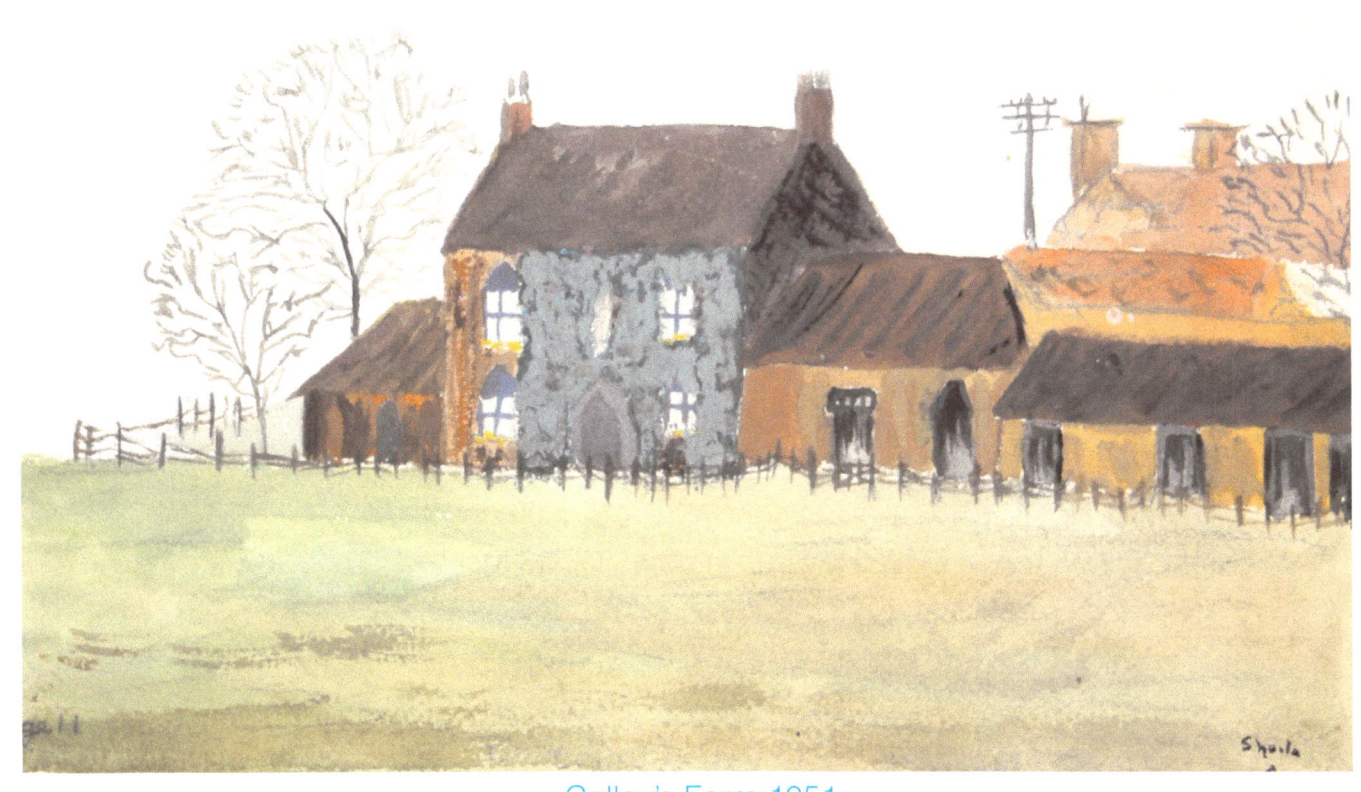

Colley's Farm 1951

For my first art homework set by "Miss Nail" we had to paint "Something we pass on the way to school." It was my Mother's suggestion to draw Colley's Farm.
Off I set five minutes walk down Grosvenor Road and sat on the fence opposite "Tyncholme" with my water colour pad and paints.

We liked Mr. Colley as he used to give us straw for our "guy" on Bonfire night.
It was sad to see his farm pulled down in the next few years to make way for the New Marine School.

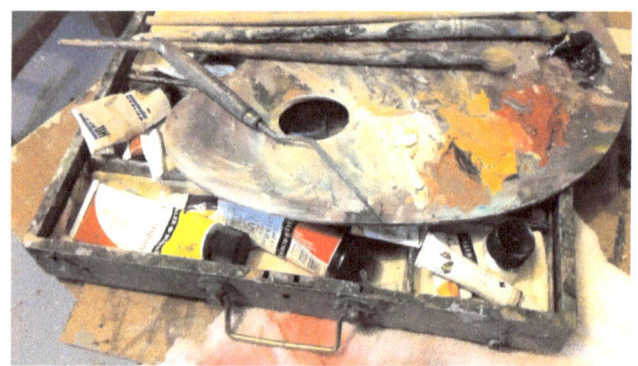
Paint Box for my 13th Birthday

For my 13th Birthday my Dad answered an ad. in the Shields Gazette for a box of Oil Paints. He was a great one for second hand stuff.

We went together to the house of an elderly lady (probably 72 like me!) who explained she had arthritis and could not paint any more, hence she was selling her paint box .
With it came all brushes, paints and even stubs of paper for charcoal rubbing which I'd never heard of before.

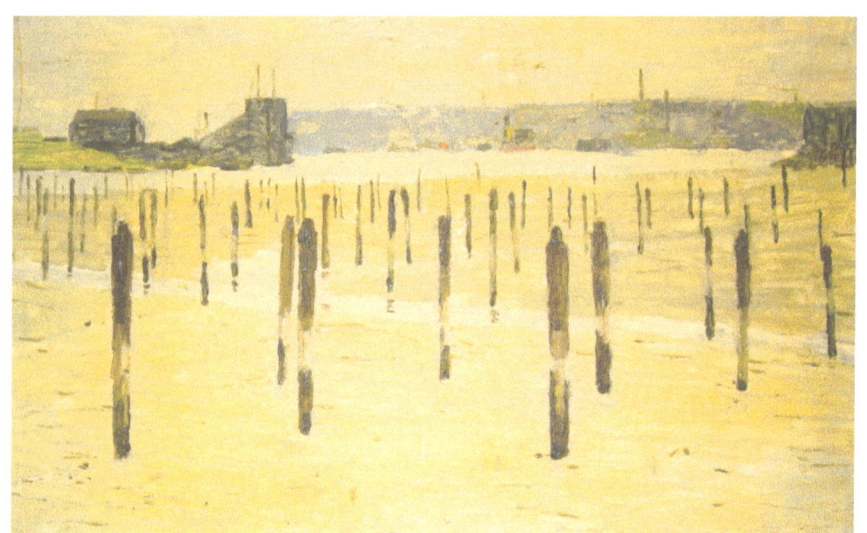
Jarrow Slake originally painted in1953
With Coal Staithes on the left.

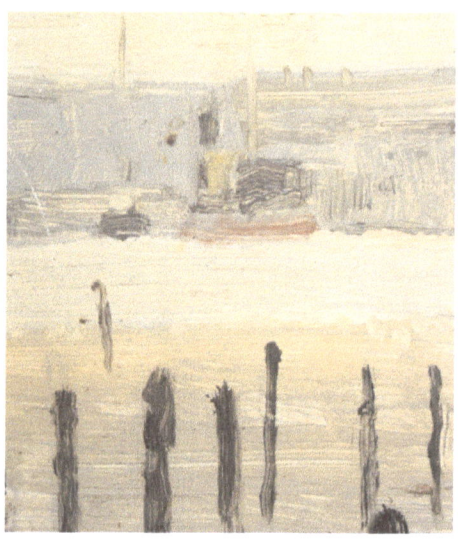
Close up view of what looks like a Lawson-Batey "Tyne-Tug: in the background.

One of the first paintings I did with it was on primed hardboard. My folks took me to Jarrow Slake where I sat on the running board of my Dad's battered Ford 8 and painted directly from life. The paints and charcoal are long gone; but I still use the box to this day.

It has great memories for me, every time I open it up to paint I still feel that first excitement I experienced when I was 13.

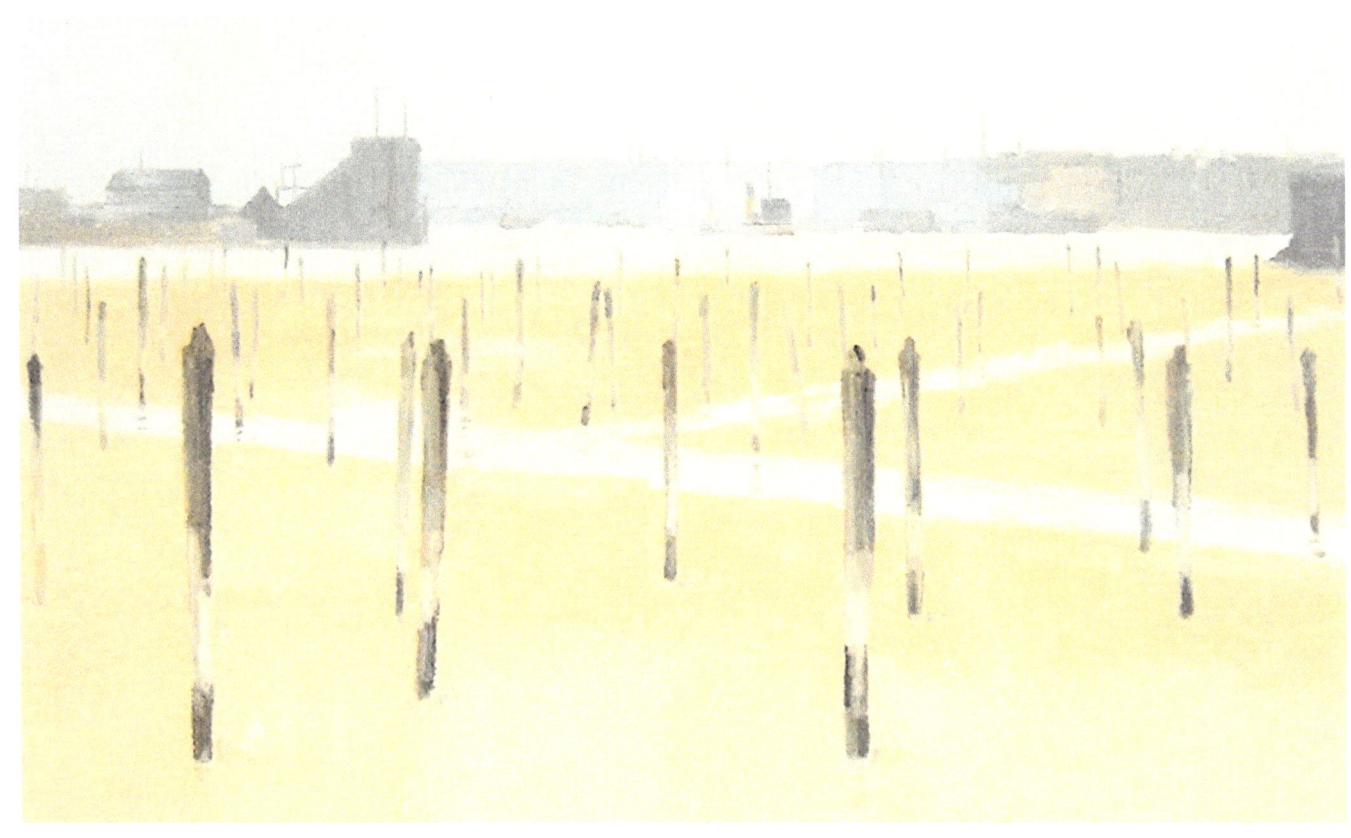

Jarrow Slake 1953 - repainted in 1974

Of all the paintings I'd done over the years Jarrow Slake was my Mother's favorite.
So I copied it in 1974 for an exhibition I held at the Gulbenkian Gallery in Newcastle in the
People's Theatre. I was, at that time, an art teacher at King George Comprehensive so many
of the Staff attended the opening. Nancy Goudie (always "Miss Goudie" to me as she used to
teach me) bought the painting. Years later when she was retired I visited her and she insisted
I take the picture back for my Mother. The next year she moved to a care home and I
realized why she had been so forceful about giving it back to me.

Thanks to her I not only had the best English teaching possible (I'm sure she'd find loads of
grammatical errors in this book!) but I still have a print of this picture to show you.

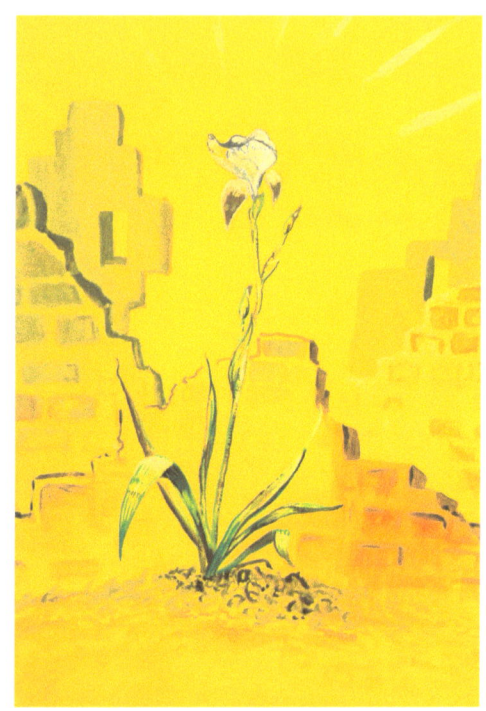

The Last Iris 1954

I'm sure we all have "premonitions" which we are not at all aware off at the time. The "Last Iris" illustrates such an event for me. Sitting on the front step of the house I can remember painting this flower as it grew in our small, but very well stocked garden.

As I worked, a thought came into my head. "What if this was the LAST iris left on the planet, and all the world had crumbled about it." So I added the make believe background not realizing that this was to be symbolic of what was about to happen to me and my family.

I was working on a wooden marquetry picture based on one of George McVay's prints of Shields, (I was always an admirer of his line drawings) when my Aunty came up the path pushing her bicycle.

She was my Dad's sister and she told us that their brother had been diagnosed with cancer . She asked if my Mother would help look after him at their home in Pollard Street.

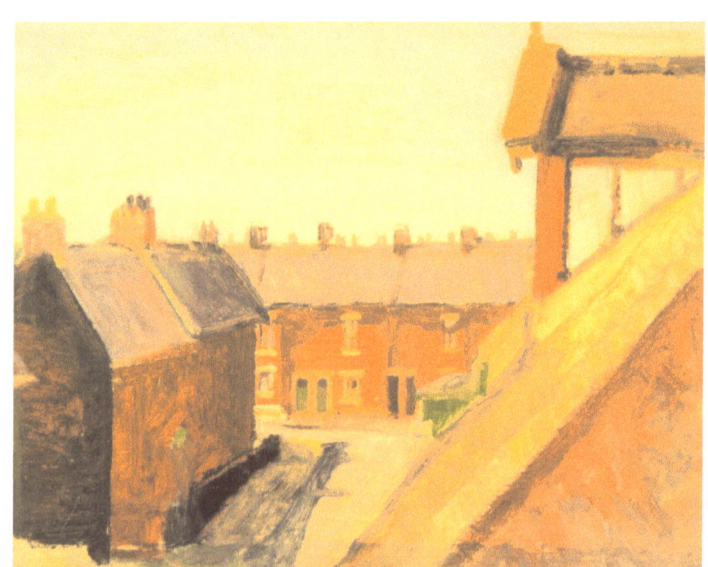

Attic Window Pollard Street 1954

We all went that week, and never came back to Lavington Road. Life can be like that.

The terrace house was really dark and dingy after the light bright home I'd been used to.

However I was lucky in having the attic as my bedroom/studio.

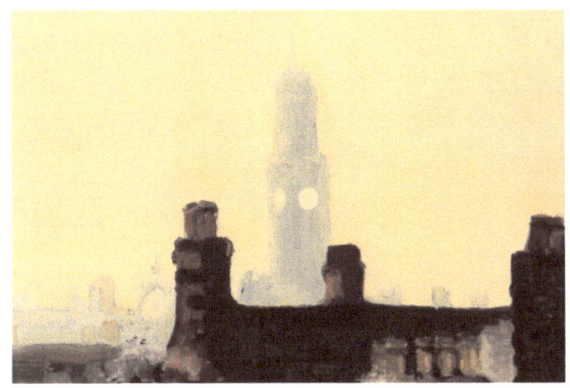

Skyline with Town Hall 1954

I painted the whole room white and splashed out onto the roof-top too. My Dad, who was, luckily for me a patient sort of chap, said "Don't worry I'll show you how to paint windows and doors properly". That painting lesson has stood me in good stead the rest of my life.

As I painted more views from the window I became very attached to skies and started to look at books on John Constable, borrowed from the library round the corner in Ocean Road.

His small sky studies are fantastic. He wrote the time of day and wind direction on the back of each sheet, evidently being very excited by a scientific book published in his day on the study of cloud formations.

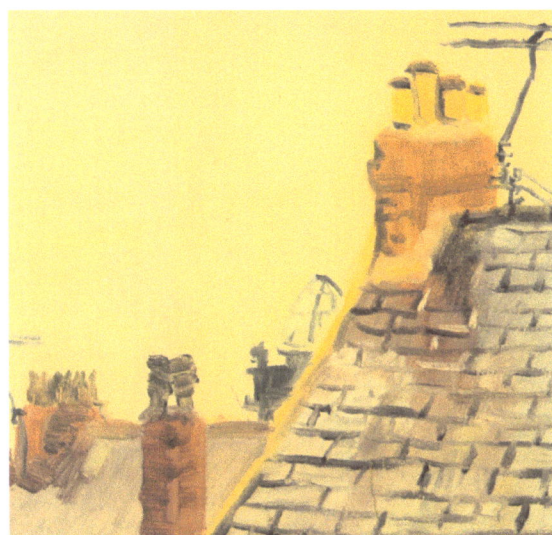

Old Marine School" Dome 1955

His enthusiasm was catching!

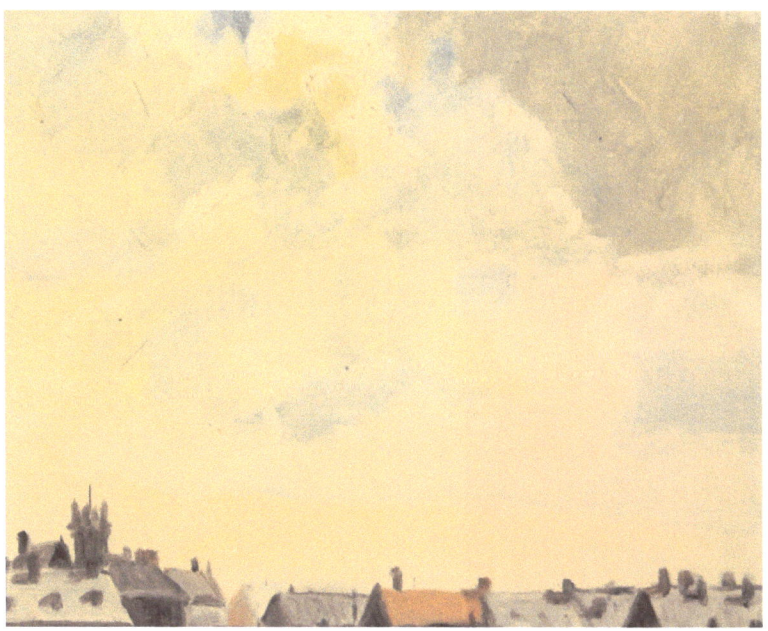

Clouds with St.John's Steeple 1956

13

My uncle died and my Aunty begged us to stay with her.

So we sold our home in Lavington Road. Shortly after this my Aunt decided that , in fact, she did not want us in her house, so we had to look for another place to stay quite quickly.

We moved just up the road to Vespasian Avenue.

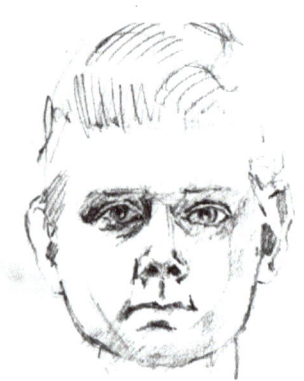

Self Portrait aged 17

It was September when we moved in and the first thing that dropped on the mat at Vespasian were my exam results. They had "well done" written on them by Mrs Ogle the the school secretary . (who was the REAL power behind the throne at the High School!)

So , I could then go on to Sunderland College of Art, just a bus ride away.

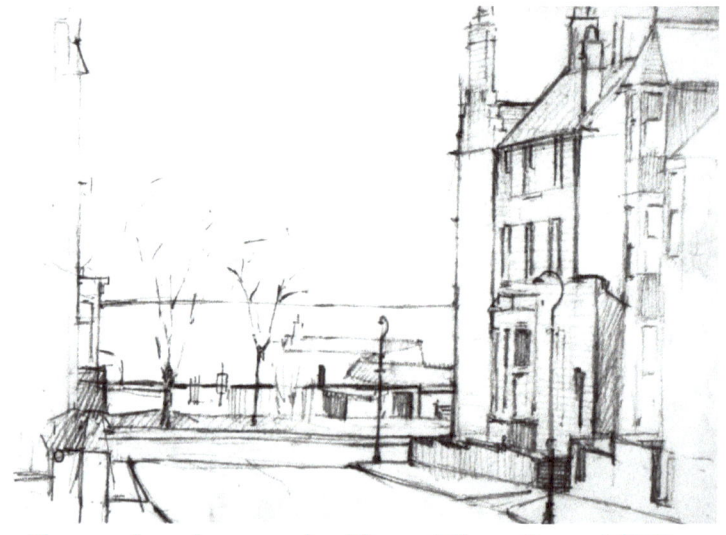

Vespasian Avenue looking at the piers. 1957

The first thing we were told was
"Forget everything we'd ever been taught"

The second was
"To look at the spaces in between"

The earlier tree on the left has texture and shading. The later trees on the right have not.

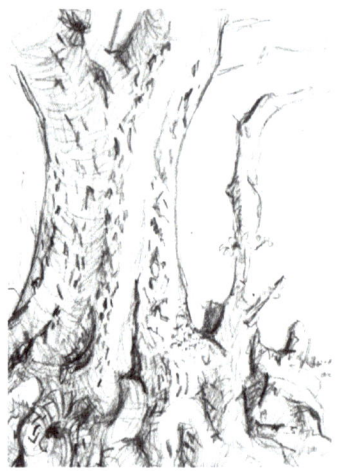

Marine Park 1957

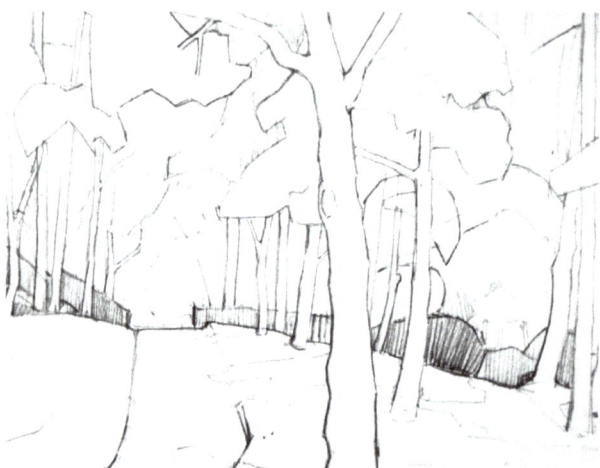

Backhouse Park, Sunderland 1958

So with my new found knowledge I started looking at the spaces in between everything about me. Starting with my own face, not a trace of shading, or emotion. Then on to all the family...

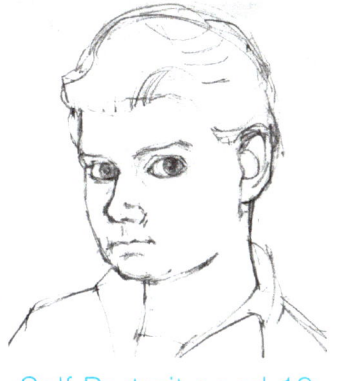

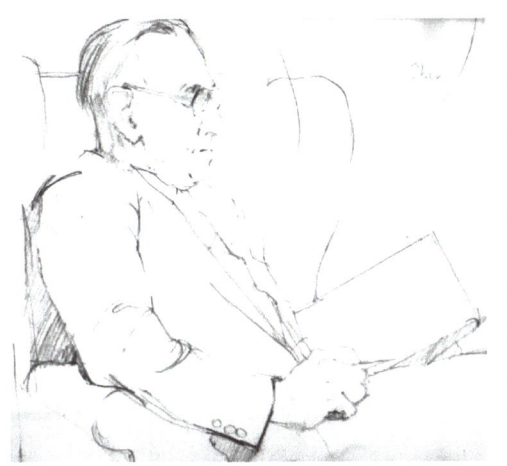

My Dad doing the Telegraph Crossword

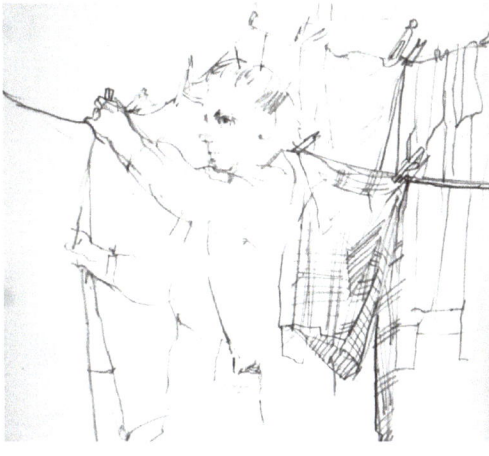

My Mam hanging out the washing in the back lane.

Self Portrait aged 18

I couldn't draw my brother as he was on National Service.

However his place was filled by my Mam's Dad who came to live with us when his wife died.

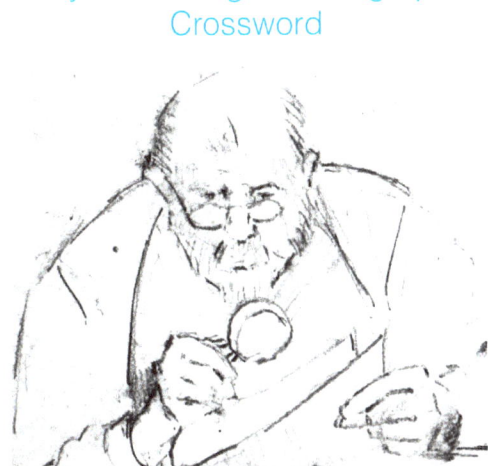

My Grandad reading .

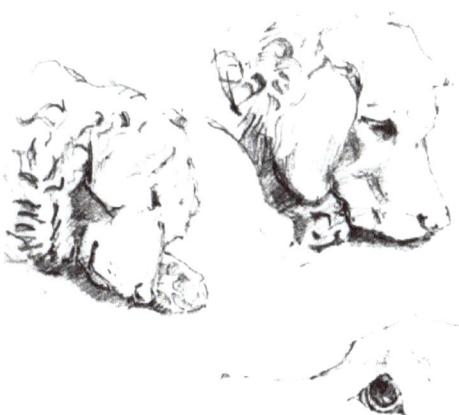

Our Golden retriever KIm. Who had been with us since this book began!

Older readers may remember her as the proprietor of "Fitzgerald's Paper Shop" in Westoe Rd.. Some say that she was a bit tough like Margaret Thatcher, but she was always fair to me. I liked her, and the comics I could read in her shop when I was younger.

So we had all arrived, by a series of "happy accidents", at the famous "Lawe Top" and were now official "Skate Enders". I know there are many reasons and spellings as to where this-term came from. My Mam said it was because the Lawe used to be an island in the shape of a skate.Years later I saw a model of the river Tyne in Roman times at the Newcastle Museum of Antiquities, sure enough there was a little flat fish shaped island at the mouth of the Tyne.

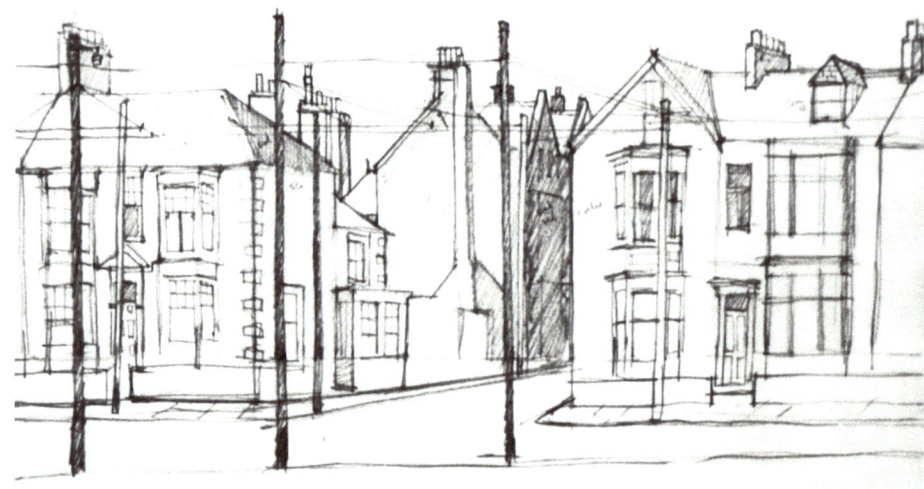

Outside I was drawing everything in sight. Here it's where Vespasian Avenue meets Lawe Road.

I seemed to have taken great care in getting the trolley bus wires to hook up accurately!

On the horizon of the Marine Park you can see a tiny castle turret.

Lawe Top with Trolley Bus Wires 1958

This was "Trinity Towers" or the " Old PIlot's Look Out". The Mother of a schoolfriend Shirley Shotton, a fellow "Skate Ender", asked for a painting of this. That made me look all the closer at my subject.

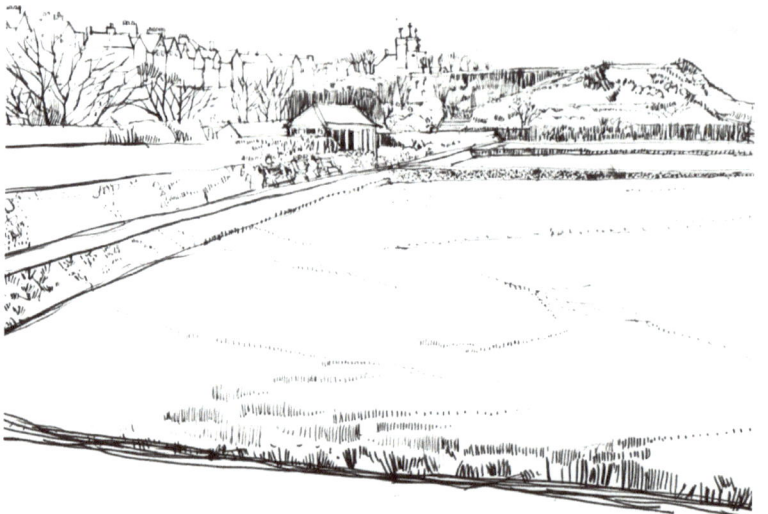

Marine Park Bowling Green 1958

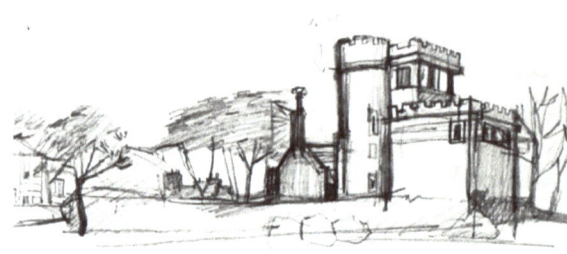

Trinity Towers1958.

A Christmas present in 1959 was a box of "Rembrandt" pastels (not second hand this time). With these I was able to travel about and use colour.

The Customs House at that time was still collecting customs from passing ships. My Dad explained that Whalers used to dock there. I took this without a flicker. A "Whaler " to me at that time was just a big ship.

Thank goodness the horrors of whaling have now been brought to our attention. We've come a long way in 45 years, and so has the Customs' House!

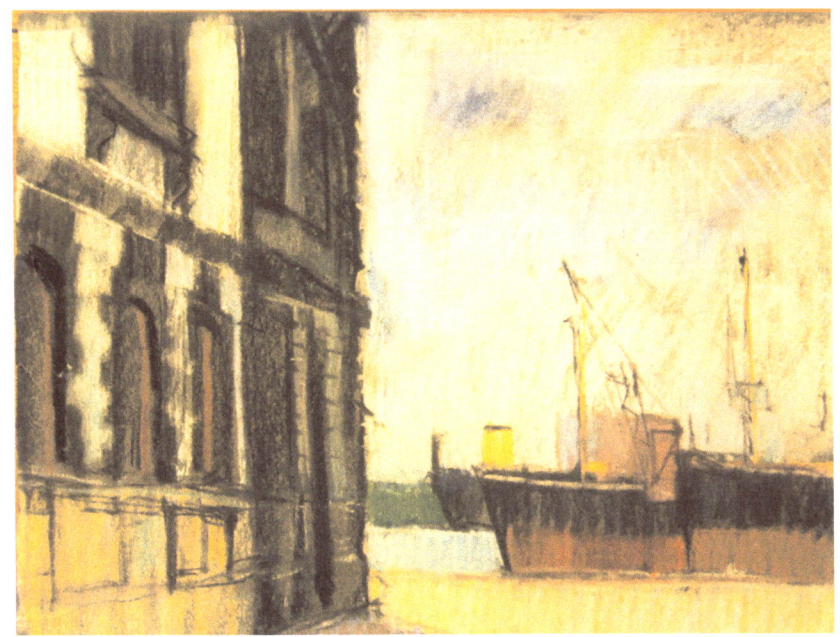

The Customs House, Mill Dam 1959

It was easy to get to Newcastle by rail from South Shields train station just up the road from us.

I drew the river a lot from the Newcastle Quayside. All the pictures I made were given away to friends and family. The only image to survive is this one of the High Level Bridge.

Sitting drawing was a good way for art students to save money, as it kept you out of the shops!

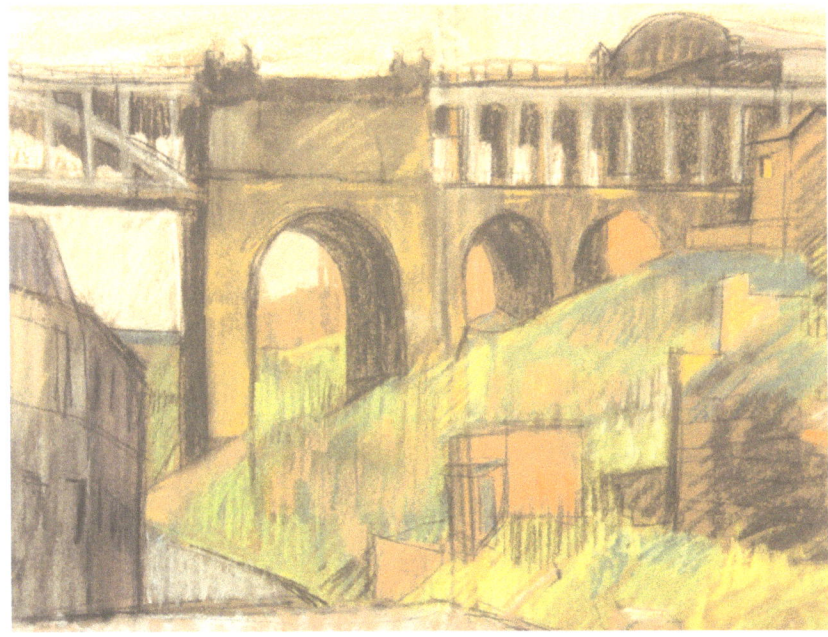

High level Bridge Newcastle Upn Tyne 1959

17

In my final year at Art College I faithfully continued "looking at the spaces in-between", and I think you can see my drawing became more accurate and clear. However it lacked any sense of emotion or purpose other than to record what was in front of me.

I thought - is this REALLY what art is all about ?

Until I found any answers to this question I continued to look at and to draw the Tyneside about me.

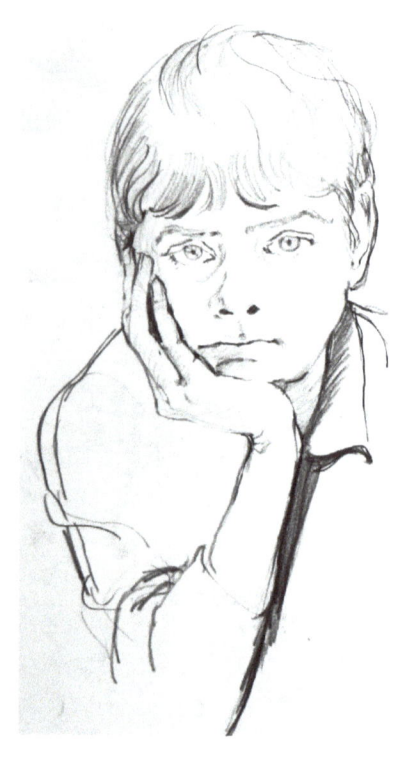

Self Portrait Aged 19

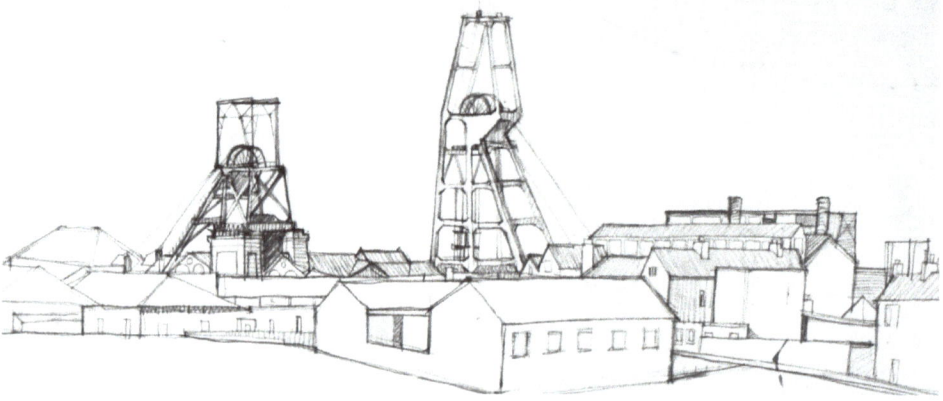

Whitburn Colliery 1959

My Mother's eldest sister Mabel did a little bit of rent collecting in her later years and one day I drove round with her as she knocked on doors. I think the doors opposite are those in South Eldon Street. The terrace is typical of many that were pulled down in later years.

Mabel was the only woman driver I'd seen up till then. She drove because her husband , who worked in the pit above as a Deputy, didn't want to drive .She put it into my mind that it was possible, role models can help at times.

I wish I'd had a role model to tell me to date and name my pictures as I made them. I'm afraid many of the dates given are an educated guess! If you plan a career in art start naming and dating now!

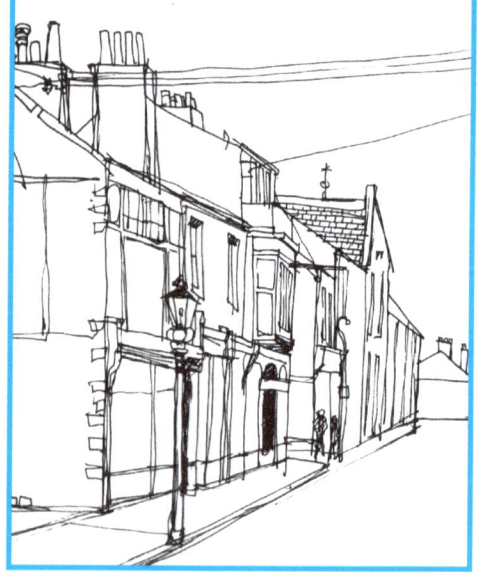

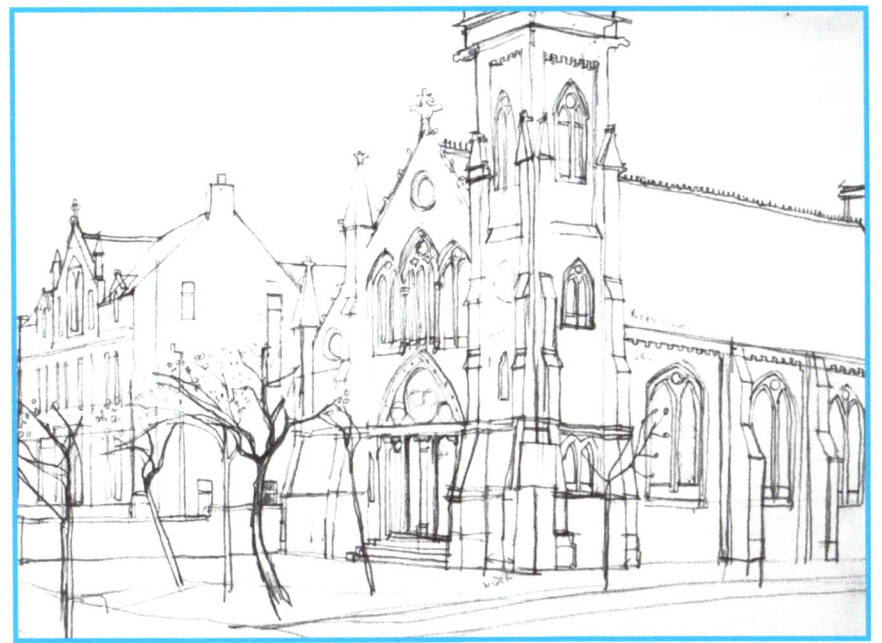

St John's Church

Churches have great shapes to draw. St. John's had extra meaning as my brother was married there in 1960.

Tombstones are dead good to draw too. I finally combined these images in a Lithograph at College.
You might spot the tiny pit head on the horizon .

These pages feel a bit glum.. and looking back I probably was. I was certainly ready for some answers, and I got them starting in the September of that year!

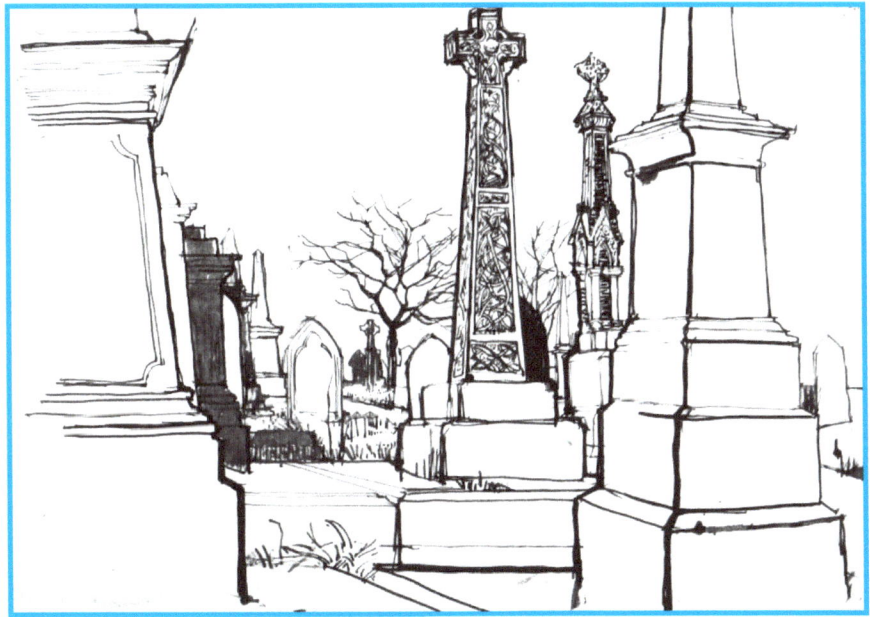

Westoe Church Yard

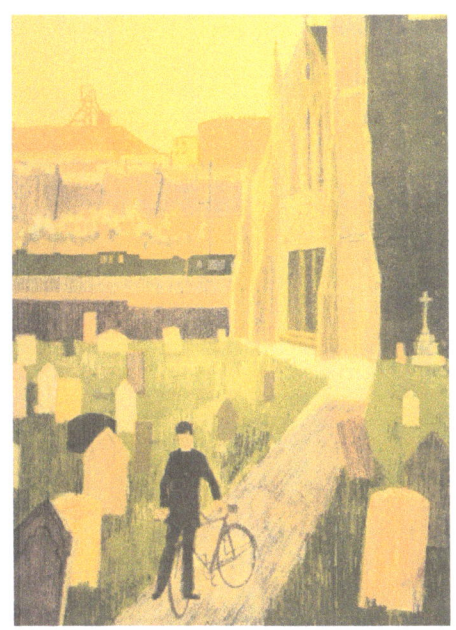

St John's Church Lithograph

Two life changing events happened in 1960

My Dad, Capt. G.W. Graber, had been appointed Pilot Master of the River Tyne since 1947. The flat above the Pilot Offices on the Lawe Top went with the job and we could have moved in at once, but my Dad said he could not leave the former Pilot Master's widow homeless. When she peacefully passed away in 1960 we moved in...

...and this was the view from my studio window!

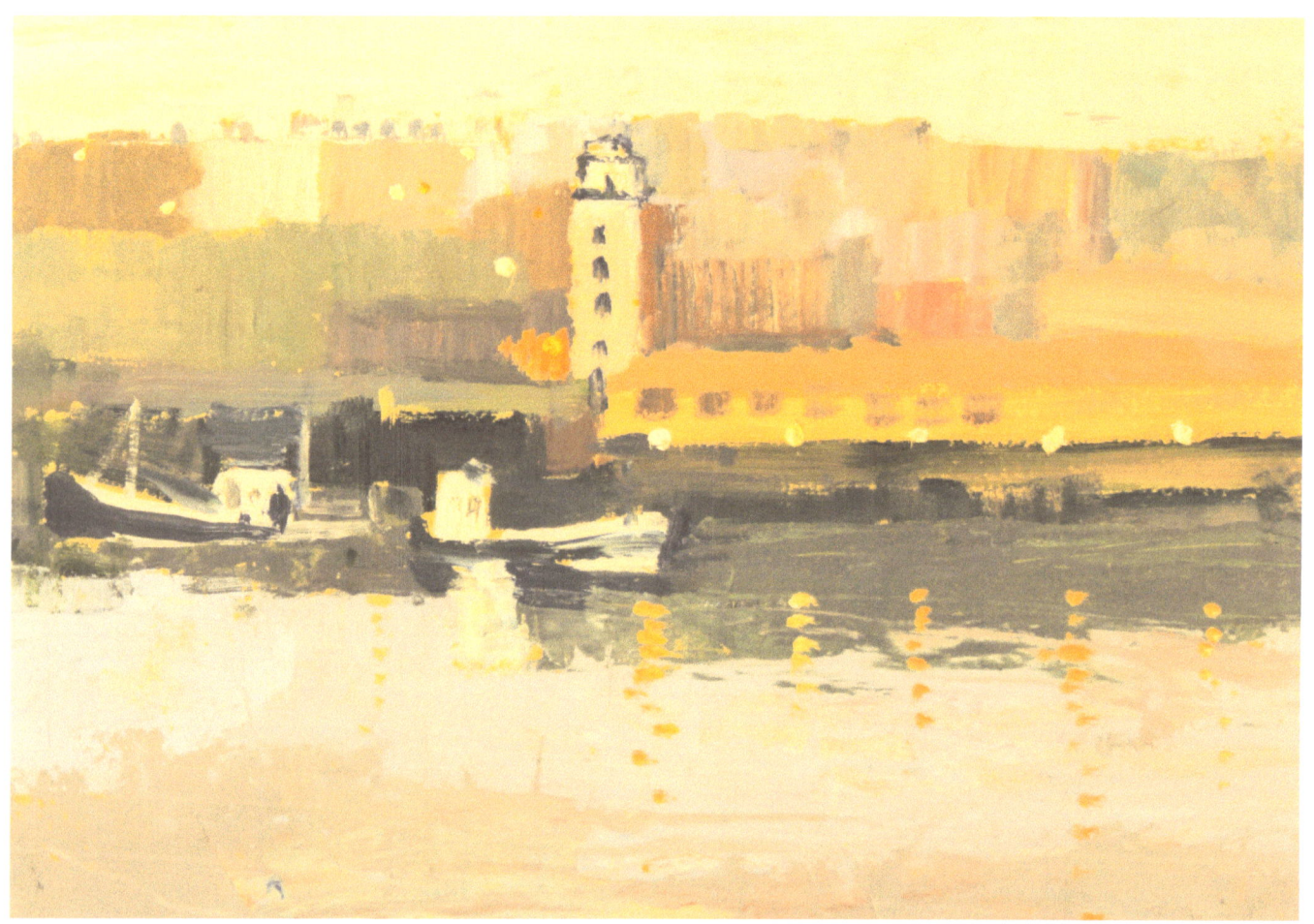

Early Evening North Shields Fish Quay 1960

I gained my National Diploma in Design which qualified me to draw with technical proficiency and little else, so I decided to apply for a teacher training course.
Fortunately I was accepted at Birmingham School for Training Art Teachers, Priory Road.
Thirty of us chatting and gasping for a smoke, waiting for our first lecture in art education to begin. In walks Mrs Burroughs a tall, grey haired figure. She stood stock still and silent.
We slowly stopped chatting and thinking about smoking.
Eventually after what seemed an age, she asked in a slow resonant voice,
"Why are you here"
Silence, then some joker spoke up "To get our Art Teacher's Diploma"
"So what is Art"
Lucy bounced back, during the rest of the course we discovered the answer for ourselves.

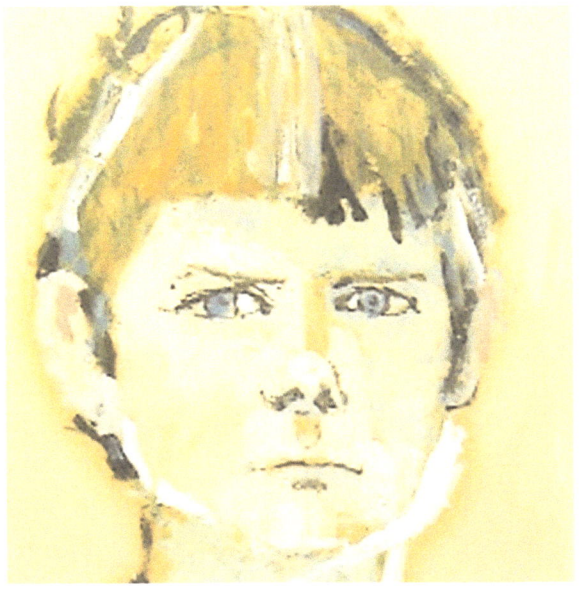

Self Portrait 1961

By working with children from Nursery to Special Needs. Visiting the noisy ,monotonous production lines on which many of them would spend their lives. We were shown that year that everyone is an artist, everyone needs to be able to succeed and express themselves in some way and it was our job as teachers of art to provide an environment from which every individual could take at their own level.

My answer had arrived and I have tried to follow it throughout my life.

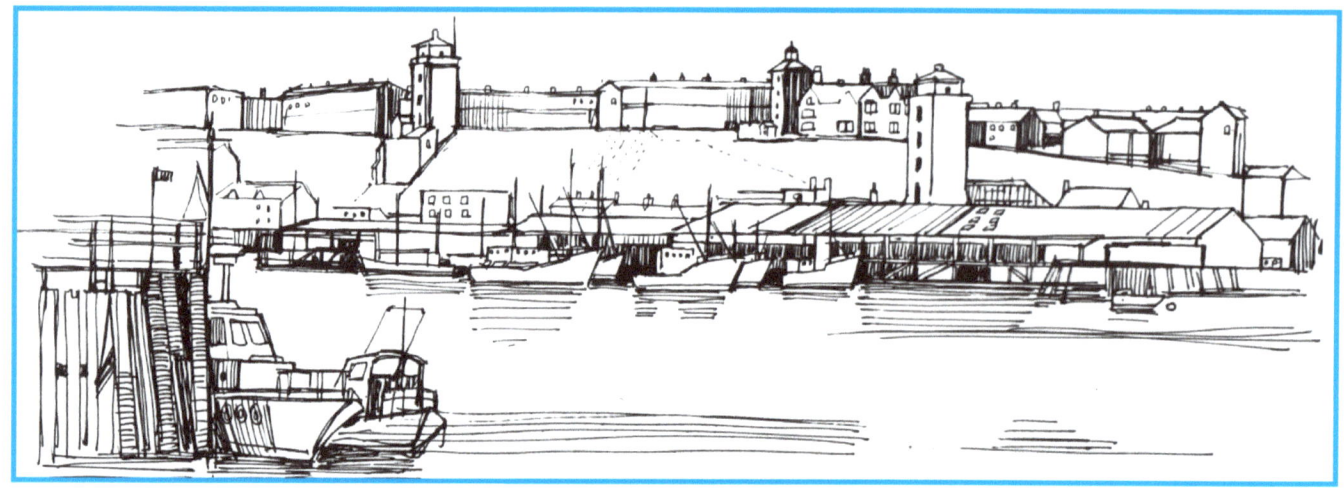

North Shields Fish Quay with Pilot's Jetty in Foreground 1960

So now we were not just visiting where my Dad worked, we were actually living there. It was literally "coming home" for me. There in front of me was the Fish Quay I'd visited from being a child when the life size wooden carving of a Fish Wife was still there and my Dad held a cod up beside me that was as big as me! The Pilot's Jetty where my brother and I had played on the Pilot Cutter and rowed the "Foy Boats" at anchor there.

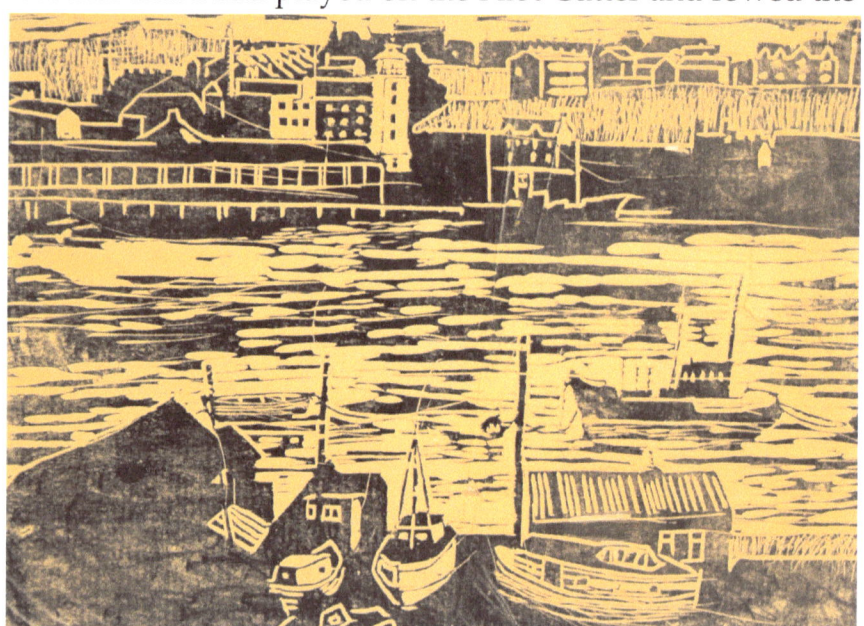

River Tyne with Boat Yard - Woodcut - 1961

The River and boat yard were always alive with activity.

The inside of the house itself had not been active at all. It was frozen in time. The whole place had an "Upstairs, Downstairs" feel about it.

In the cellar a huge dusty kitchen range, in the attic rusty victorian iron bedsteads.

The corridor walls were "institutional" in their green gloss paint below, cream above with dividing black stripe.

22

Everytime I returned at an end of a term from Birmingham the house was lighter and brighter.The main rooms were amazing in their size and plasterwork ceilings. The views of the river were stunning from all windows. I had the huge luxury of a bedroom at the back of the house overlooking a big garden and a studio at the front, magic!

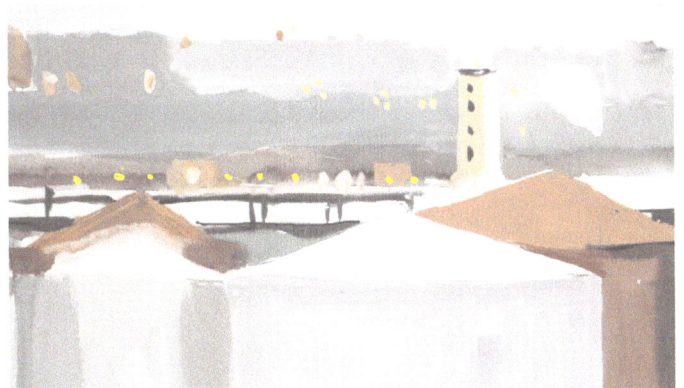 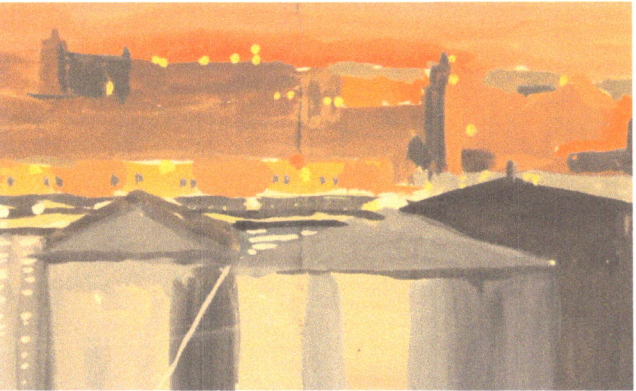

Esso Oil Drums and Low Light 1961

I found even Oil Drums could be magic too, under the right light. The images you see here were all studies for larger paintings which I don't hold anymore. I had access to reasonably priced ships canvas, which I stretched on my own wooden frames (once again my Dad showed me how) and loads of white lead paint ! Yes white LEAD, I should be dead really. So I was able to paint on large canvases, many well over six foot in length. It's amazing what a dedicated space, and a view, can allow you to create.

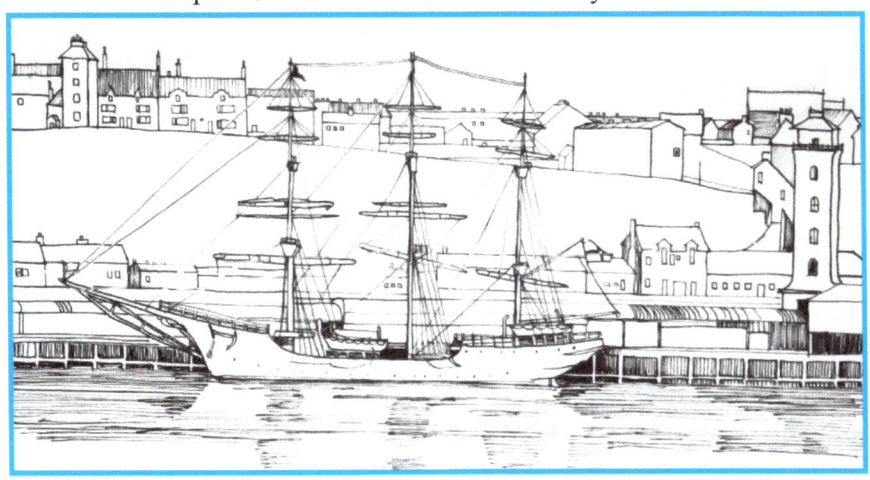

Christian Radich Norwegian Training Ship 1961

When the Christian Radich docked briefly across the river I rushed for pen and paper. As I drew I remembered when my Dad, in his civvies and I aged 13, went aboard her on an "open day". A cadet showed us round explaining what portholes etc. were. Afterwards I asked why he hadn't said he was a Captain and new all about ships. "There are times when you just listen" he said.

23

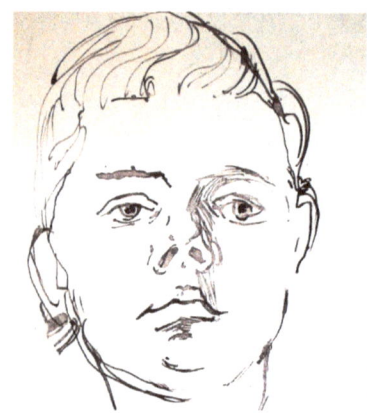

Self Portrait in Quill Pen 1962

My first job in Sept. 1961 was as an art teacher at Stanhope Road Secondary School. I had a tough time of it at the beginning as caning was the rule, as in all schools at that time. If you didn't cane then you were "soft" and had discipline problems. After a term of dissaray in the classroom I decided to actually try out the theories I'd been shown at Birmingham. They worked!

Here's one example of how.

I'd always admired the energetic pen & ink studies of Leonardo da Vinci in his notebooks as he studied the world about him.

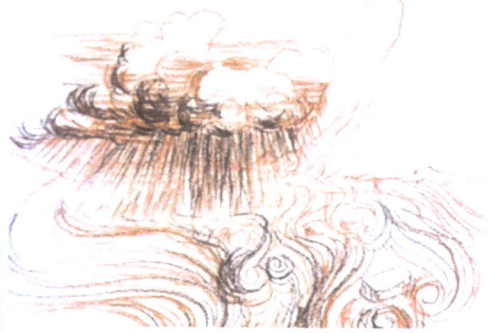

Study for a Storm from My Animated Film on Leonardo 1982

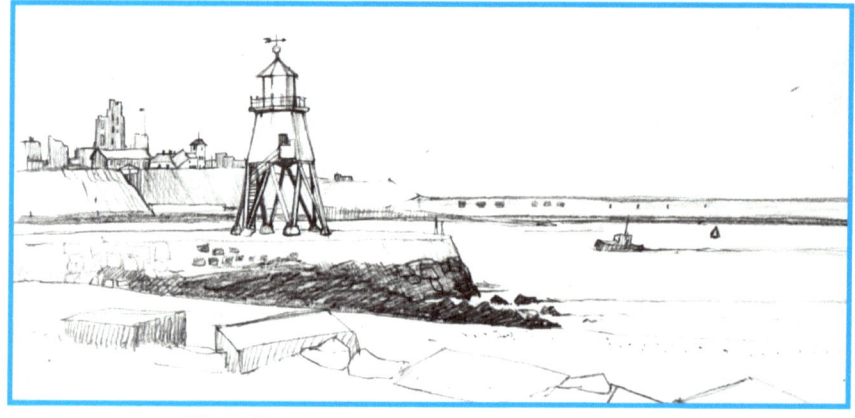

The Groyne , pencil drawing 1962

As I walked along the Groyne I picked up a seagull feather thinking I might make a pen out of it.
So I did. By sharpening the end to a point and then splitting The quill .worked surprisingly well.

I gathered a whole heap of feathers and took them in to school. Every pupil had the opportunity to carve their own knib and then have a go at drawing with it.

After showing the Leonardo drawing and my own, I played stormy music (The ride of the Valkries) on my old record player I'd taken in especially. Then suggested everyone draw their own storm their way. For the first time there was silence in class, apart from the music. The results were amazing. If there is any ex-Stanhope pupil out there with a "Stormy" picture I'd love to see it.

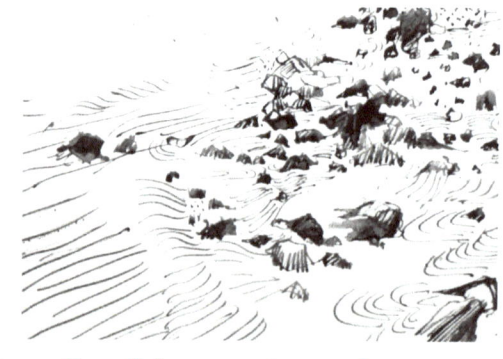

Detail from rocks at Groyne Quill Pen 1962

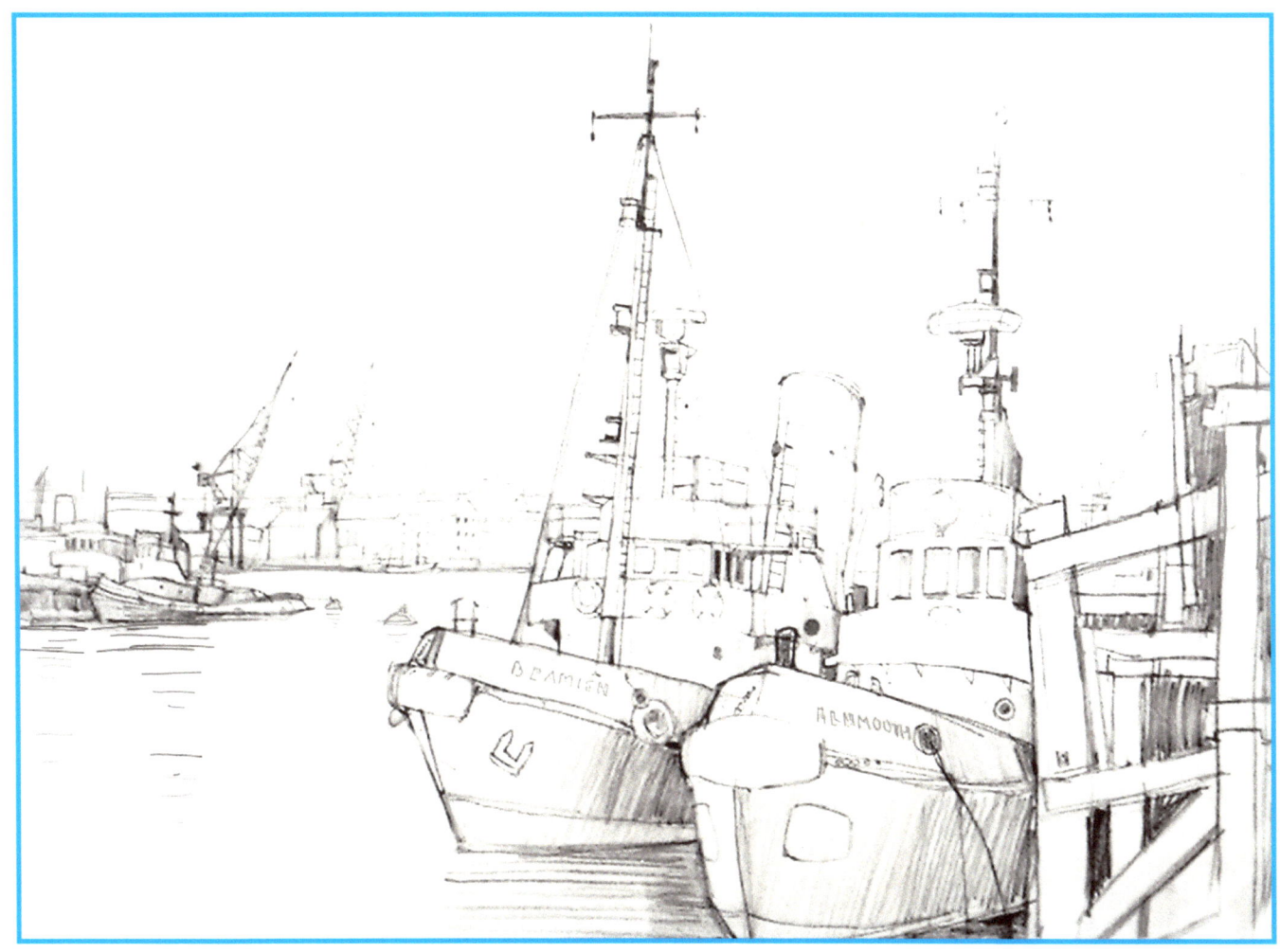

Tyne Tugs "Alnmouth" and "Beamish" anchored at the Mill Dam 1962

At weekends I'd head down to the river with my A1 Drawing board and catch any of the life I could. I just loved the shapes, sounds and smells of ships, must be the tarry rope!

Ships go back a long way for me . My earliest memory is when I was five with my Mother and brother on my Dad's Merchant Ship down in Falmouth on VE night. I didn't know what was happening other than there were some great fireworks and we had a whole bar of Cadbury's chocolate EACH!

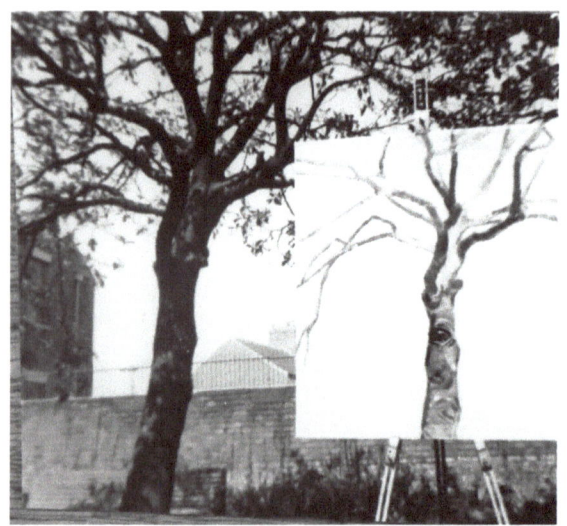

In the large garden at the back of the
Pilotage was a fantastic beam tree.
I woke up to it every morning and
painted and drew it in all seasons.

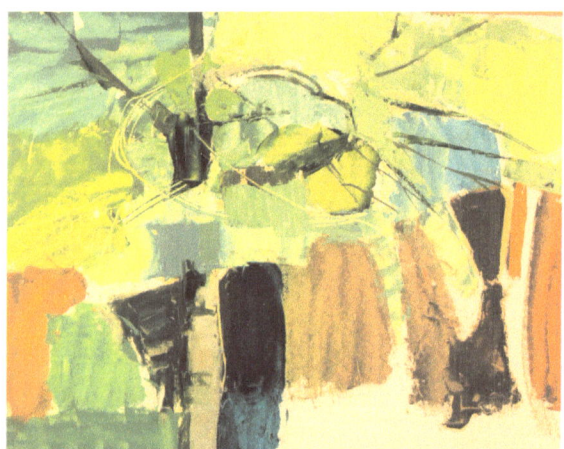

I'd got a bit carried away in the palette
knife painting above. Evidently my
Dad had said to my Mam as I worked..
*"Only God and Sheila know what she is
doing."*

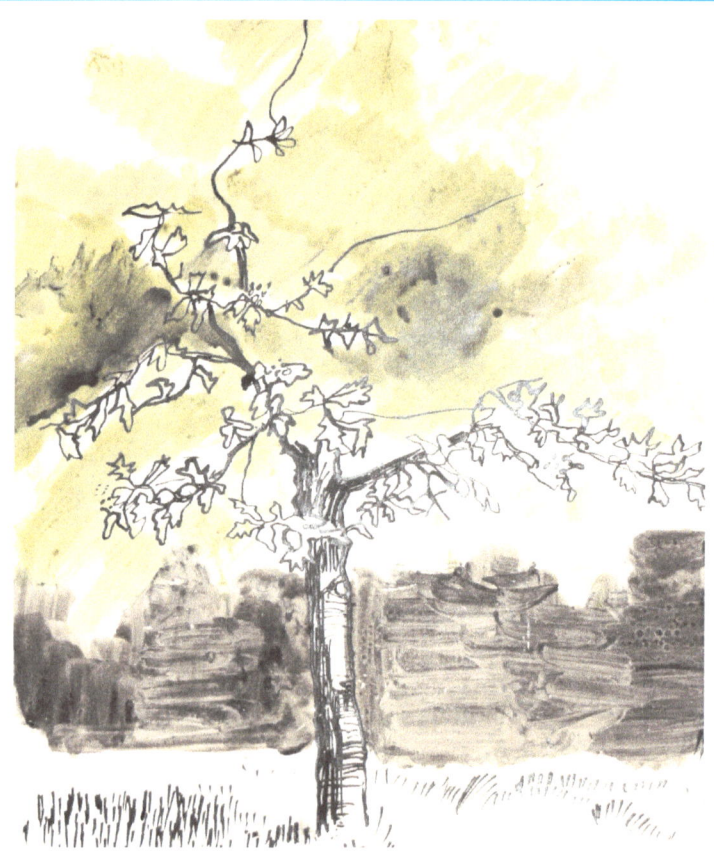

I was also reading loads of Science Fiction, like
the "Day of the Triffids", and had discovered
there was much more to Wordsworth than a
bunch of Daffs..
edited clip from his "Tintern Abbey"

And I have felt
A presence that disturbs me .. .
Of something far more deeply interfused,
Whose dwelling is the light of setting suns,
And the round ocean and the living air,
And the blue sky...and rolls through all things.

Perhaps I was breathing in too much salt air!

26

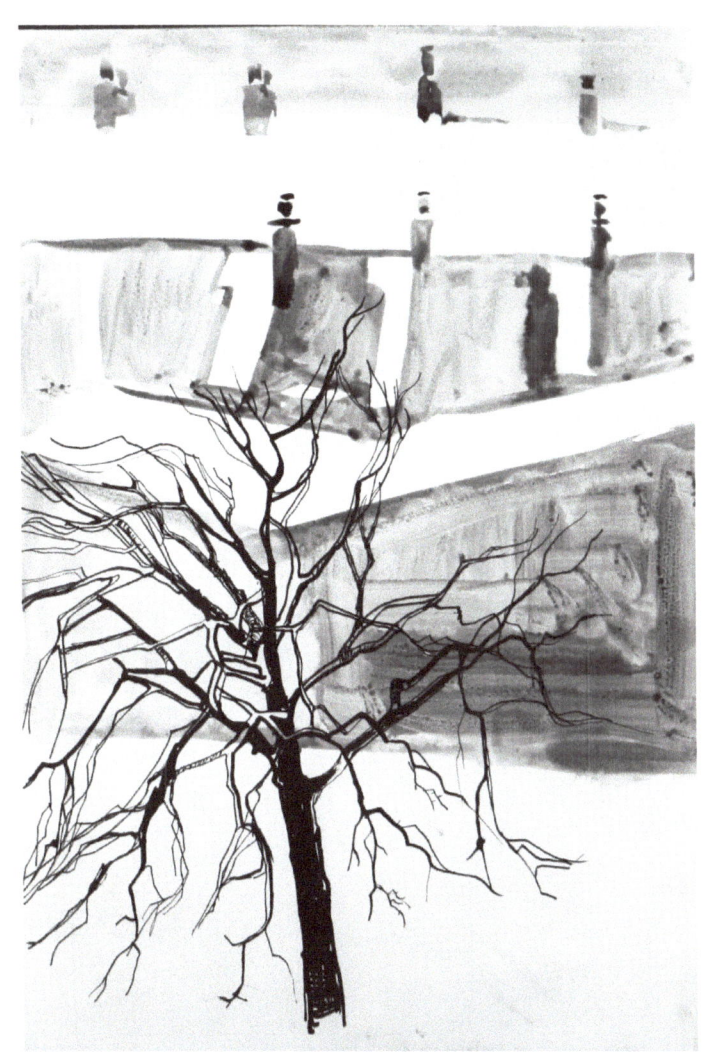

On New Years Eve 1963
my Dad died of lung cancer.

A memorial service was held at
St Stephen's "The Sailor's Church"
where the pilot's "Whale Voiice Choir"
fittingly sang "Eternal Father strong to save
whose arm doth bind the restless wave."

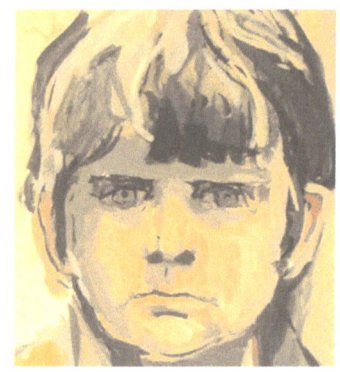

Self Portrait 1964

The house was still full of flowers when I was surprised by a chap coming up the stairs carrying a table.

The new Pilot Master was moving in. It was, after all a tied house and went with the job.

My Mother and I were lucky in finding a Council Flat very quickly. The hardest part when downsizing is deciding what to keep and what to throw away.

Somehow most of these pictures survived packed in a wooden "Toy Box" Dad had made for us. years ago.

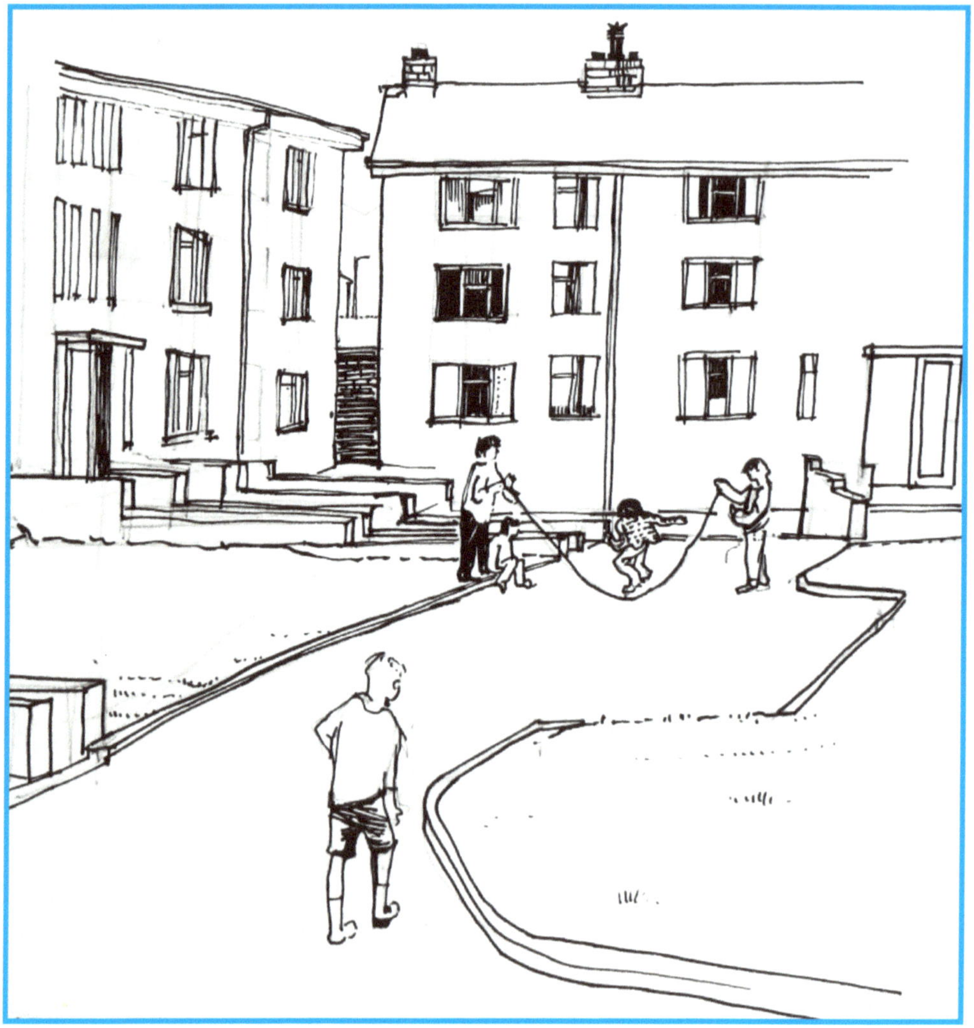

View from our Downstairs Flat at River Drive 1964

The plus side of moving to a smaller place for me was it was so much easier to put the milk bottles out at night. At the Pilotage it was quite a scary trip going down the wide stairs past the dark cellar steps where anyone could be hiding. Stick the bottles hastily outside the huge double doors and race back up.

In our downstairs flat I could practically lean out of bed and do it!

There was a lot of activity in my life from 1964 -69 but I have few Tyneside images to show for it. I was engaged to a sea going chap whom I had known from my early teens. He was a friend of the family and we met when he was studying for his tickets at the local Marine School. In 1965 we were married and lived at Sunniside Drive. I was now teaching art in the annex in Mowbray Road at South Shields High School for Girls.

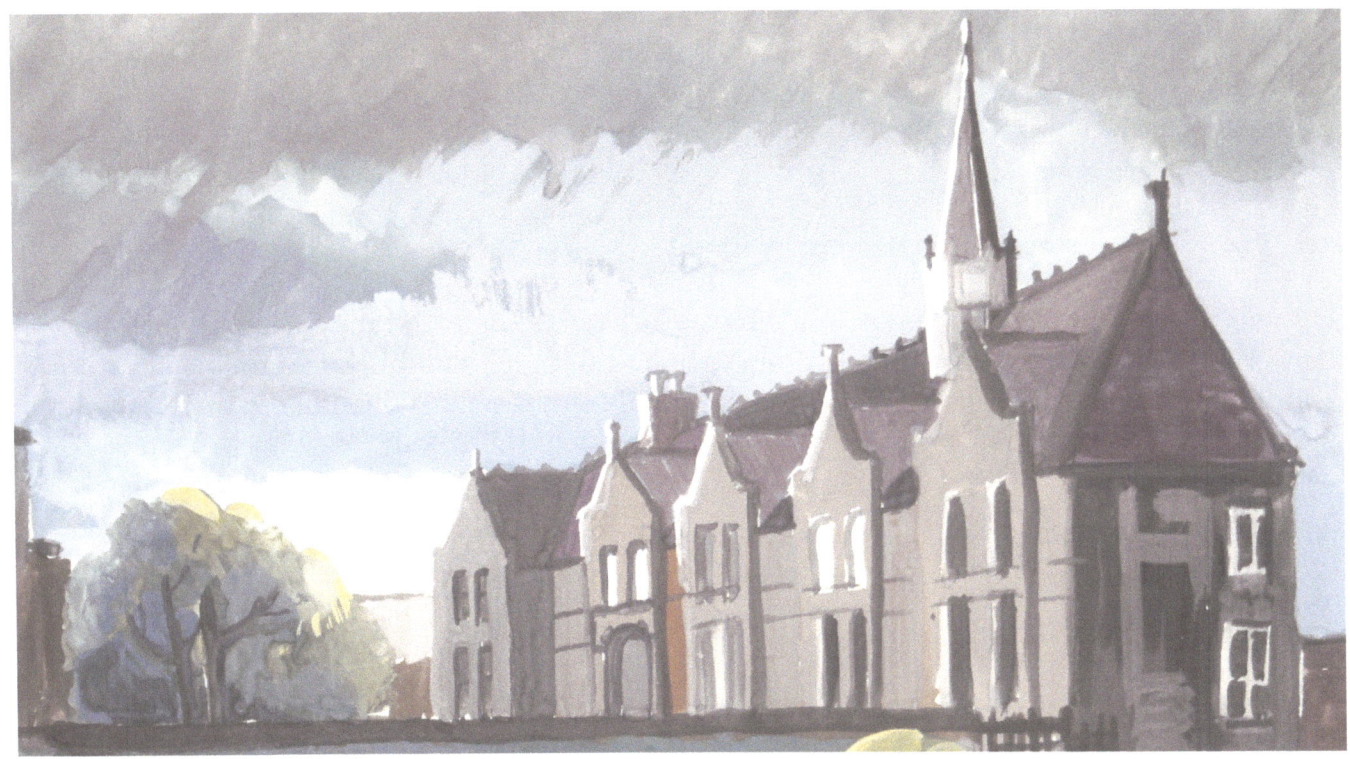

Sketch for painting of "The Old Art School Building " Mowbray Road 1968

In 1968 my Headmistress Dr. Ramsden retired. I had known her as a neighbour back in Lavington Road when our ball went over the fence to her garden . She politely let us in to collect it. Because of that early kindness, and also because she had been a really good Head. I painted her a picture of the "Old Art School Building" as a leaving present.

I eventually jumped ship and was divorced. realizing that civilized Cruise Ship life was not for me. The ship was too big and didn't smell of tarry rope! I felt much more at home teaching and painting. Maybe Aldous Huxley was right saying :-

" *An intellectual is someone who has discovered something much more interesting than sex*"

Returning to live with my Mam in her single person's flat I slept in a sleeping bag on the floor. Anyone who has lived in those flats will know that the trendy "underfloor heating" did not heat. I hope it does now!

One of of those events then happened that only occur in books... ah yes this IS a book.!

My Dad's elder brother Bill had gone to live in America when young and became an architect.

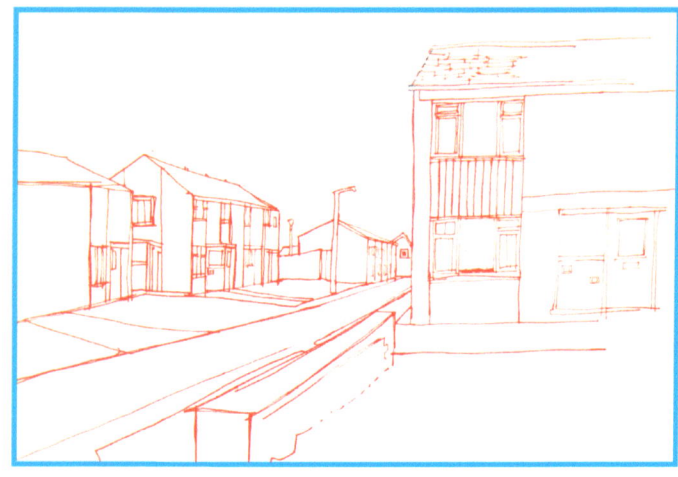

View from Biddick Hall Downstairs Flat 1969

He sent us a "ViewMaster Stereoscopic Viewer" in the 1950's when they were unheard of here. We must have looked at the two reels we had with it, "Bambi" and "Yellowstone Park" a million times. He also posted copies of "National Geographic" which had a huge impact on me as, at that time, there was few magazines or books in full colour.

When he died his estate was divided between all the family. My Mother and I received enough to put a deposit down on 50 Meldon Avenue. So thanks Uncle Bill, you changed my life for the better at many levels, and we never even met.

Space and freedom again at last! As soon as we moved in I dashed upstairs to paint whatever view was there.

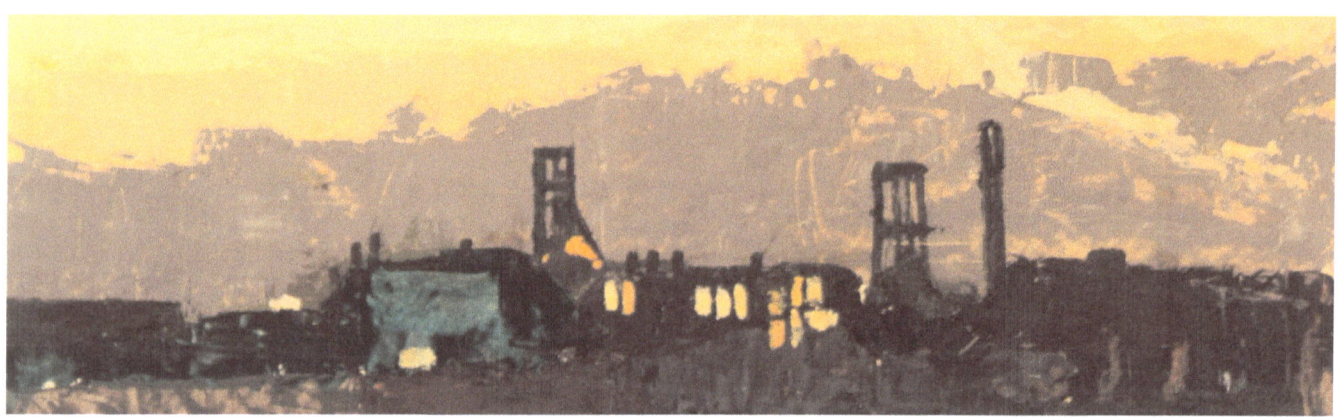

View from Back Bedroom Window at Meldon Avenue, overlooking Boldon Colliery

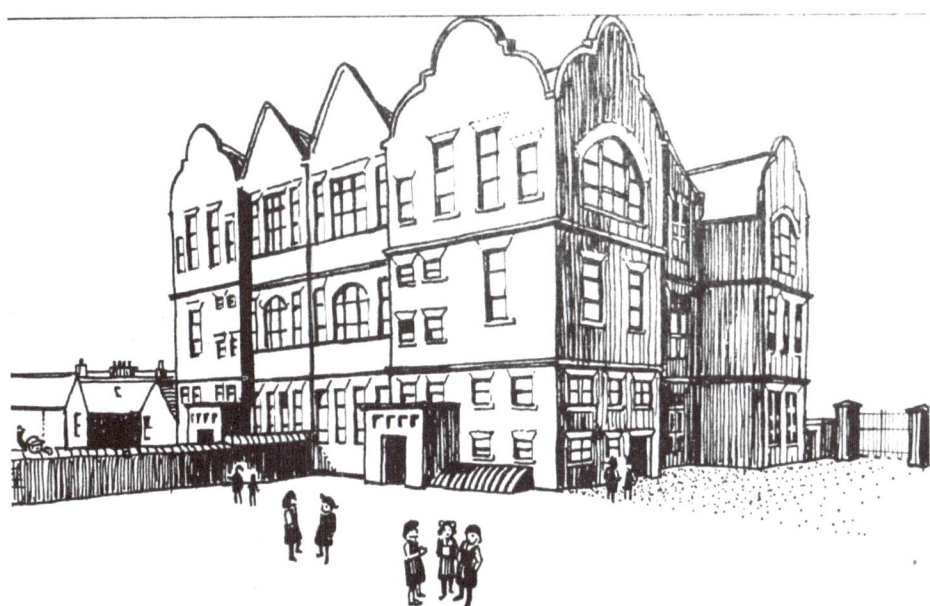

Higher Grade Mixed School 1902, became High School for Girls, then Grammar Technical School for Girls, then Grammar School for Girls. Now demolished.

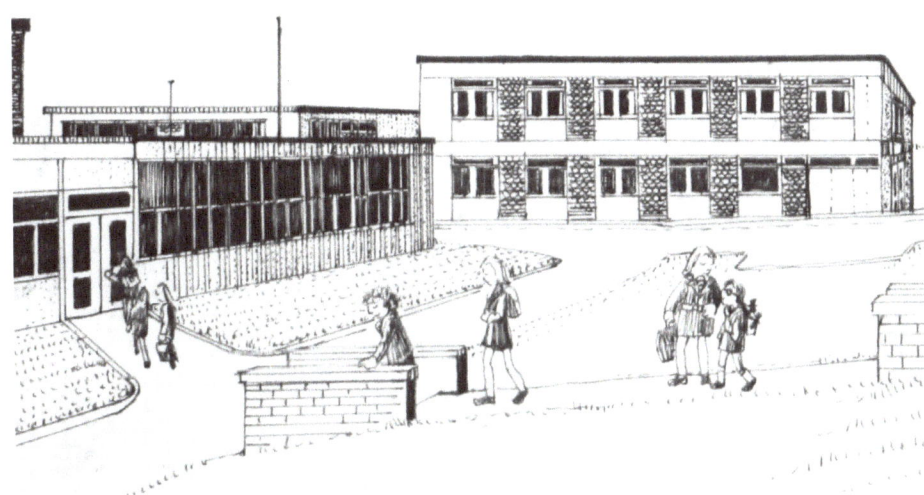

King George School for Girls 1972,
Became King George Comprehensive School, then
King George V School. Demolished 2007

The School Building in Iolanthe Terrace had a varied century.

interesting that it began as a mixed school, became all girls, moved to King George Road to eventually change back to a mixed school.

In 1972 I did these drawings as a memento for the school magazine. "The Chronical"

Miss Harris, the Headmistress was an accomplished water colour artist herself, always making studies as she travelled the world. Hence she really appreciated the importance of art as a key subject on the curriculum.

I was given a free hand to design a large open plan department in which our team of four taught art, pottery, stage design and fabric printing . Enabling everyone in the school to have a go at some aspect of art up to exam level or just for fun.

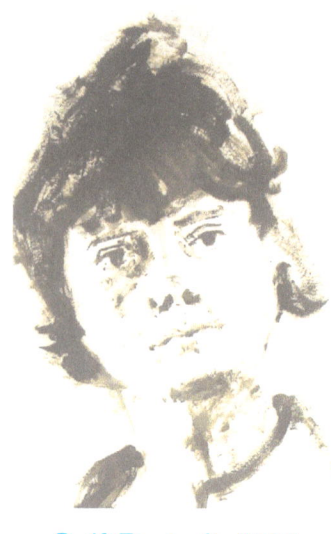

In 1970 whilst working at the Old Art School in Mowbray Road I received a phone call asking if there was anyone there who could make a seal. I thought, well yes, I'll have a go at that. I'd done a bit of calligraphy so thought I could stick a fancy seal on the end if needed. It turned out to be the Noble organization and they required a life size, "kiddies ride" type of model seal!

Ooops... however I had a go and with chicken wire and plaster. In a corner of the air raid shelter know as the "pottery hut" at Mowbray Road created a seal that they then cast in fiberglass.

I went on to make several animals in the garage at Meldon Avenue. With the fee given I bought a super 8 cine camera and started playing with animation. This eventually led to a full time career. Just goes to show your fate is never really "sealed" if you're willing to explore something new.

Especially if it's by accident!

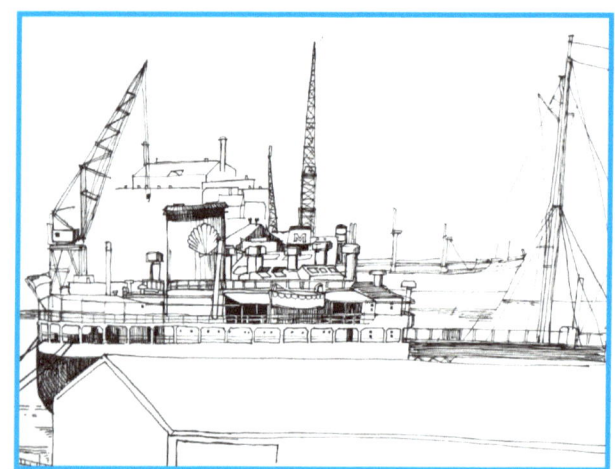

Shell Tanker pen & Ink

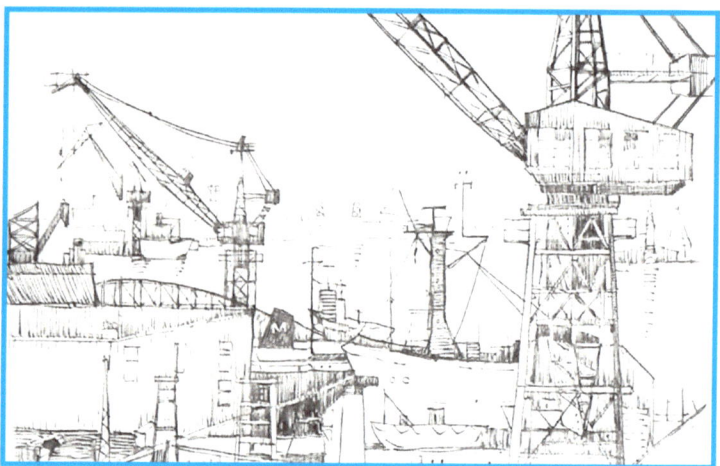

River Tyne with Ferry Landing

My day job was teaching but in the evenings I was still "drawn" literally to the river. I'd take my drawing board with paper pinned firmly down against the wind. Sit in a place I could balance my bottle of ink and get drawing. From those studies I would make large oil paintings at home, now on hardboard, the heady days of cheap canvas were over!

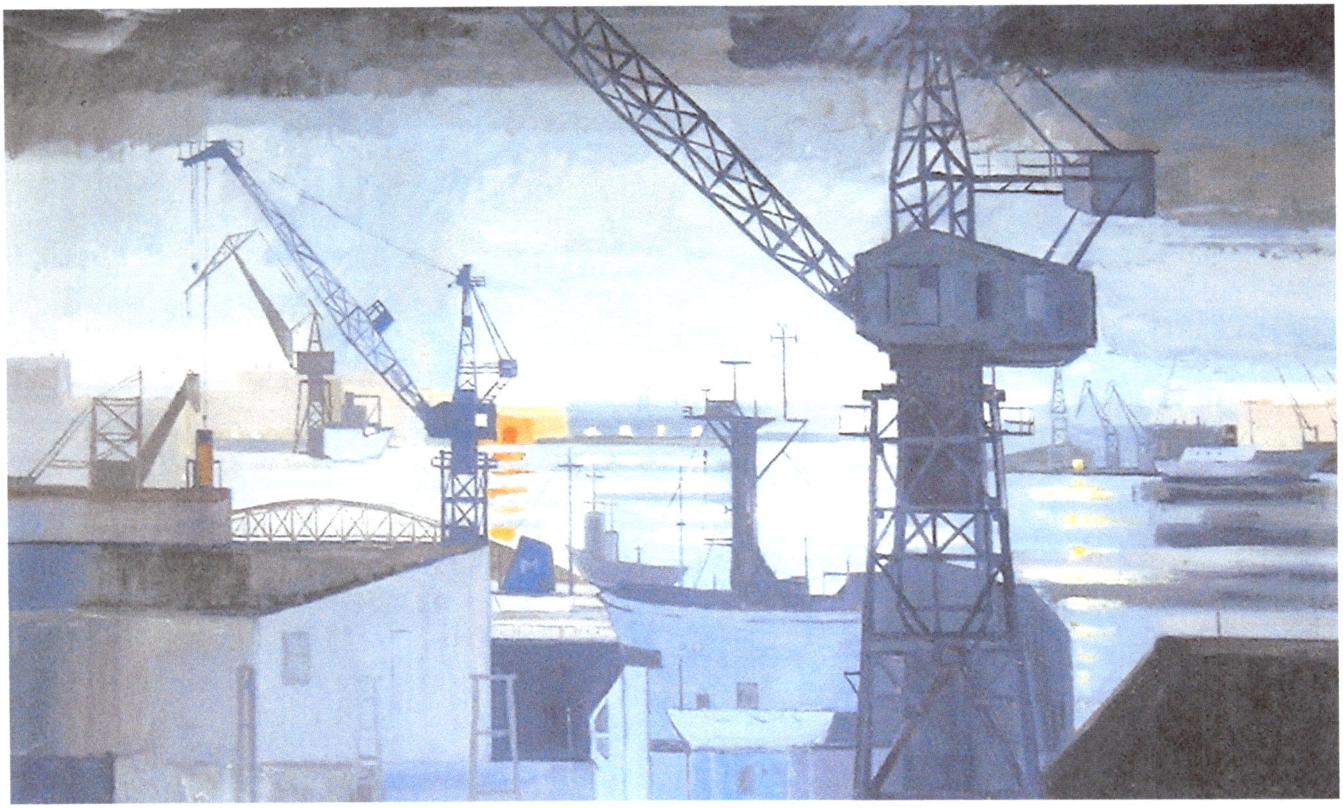

River Tyne with Ferry Landing, Mill dam and Coal Staithes in distance

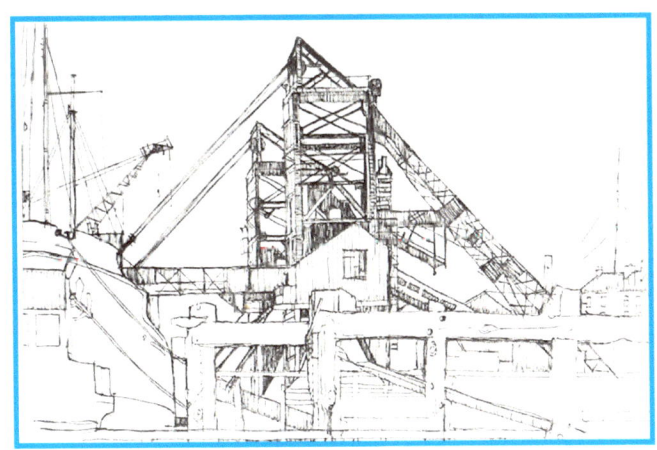

Mill Dam pen & Ink

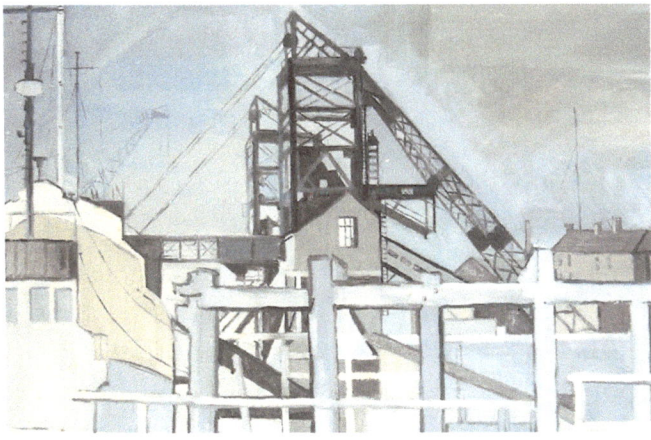

Mill Dam oil paint on board

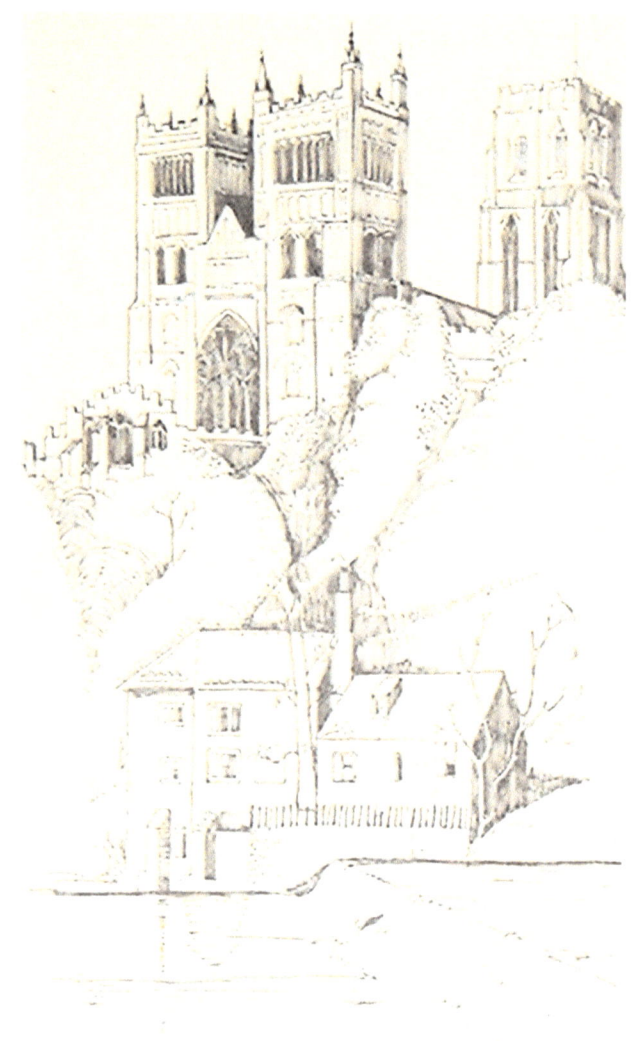

Durham Cathedral pen & ink

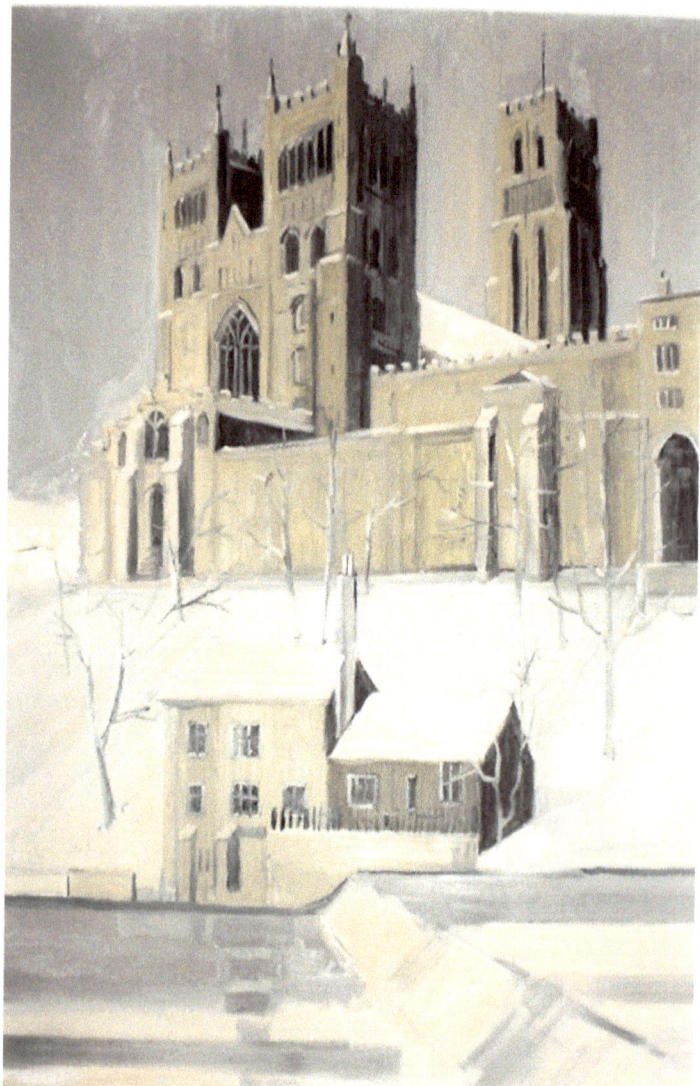

Durham Cathedral in Winter

I was also attracted to other buildings and sites in and around Tyneside. As I said earlier churches are strong shapes to draw, and they don't come much stronger than Durham Cathedral. By 1973 I had created quite a large body of work, stacked up in my spare bedroom.. A friend suggested I might approach the Gulbenkian Gallery in Newcastle People's Theatre for an exhibition. In 1974 I exhibited there. I'd like to think that someone reading this still has a painting bought at that show, please e-mail me if you do, for old times sake!

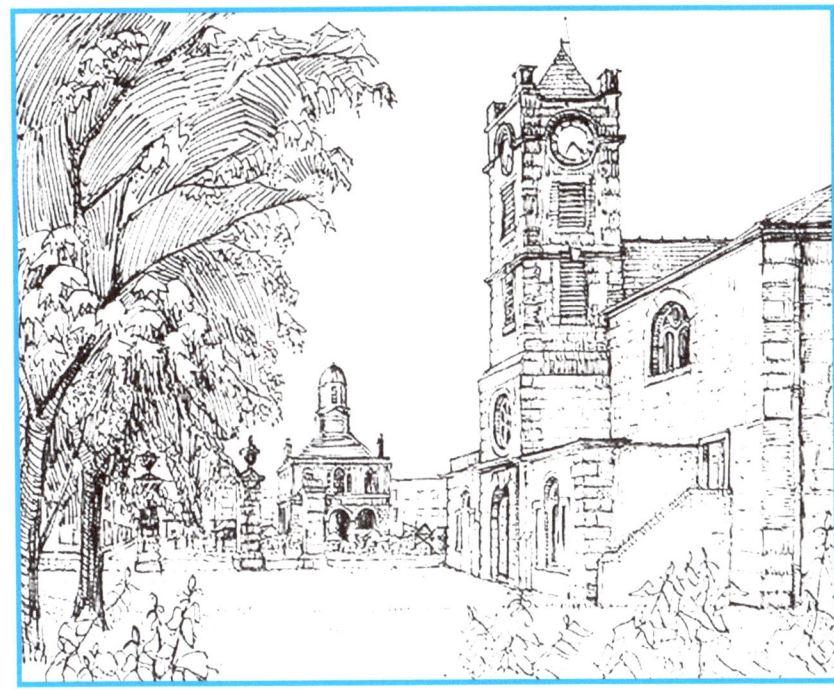

St Hilda's Church with Old Town Hall

My Mother's Grandad had a chain of herbalist shops in Shields. One opposite St Hilda's Church. She worked at "Hunt THe Herbalist" in her teens and met my Dad there when he was a cadet and looked in from his ship docked nearby for a Glass of Hunt's Herbal Beer.

Sadly John Hunt's only son Lieu. Colonel John W. Hunt was killed in World War 2 aged 44. Evidently his Dad lost all interest in his shops and let them run down and close. However in the Market Place shop he still supervised the mixing of his famous "Blood MIxture". "Put in 5 lbs of Epsom Salts Miss" he said to my Mam. "But Sir that's far too much, remember we are working to smaller quantities now". However, relieved customers returned for more, as "That was the BEST Blood Mixture ever".

All I know about Trinity is "At Trinity Church I met my Doom". Maybe you know the story behind that?

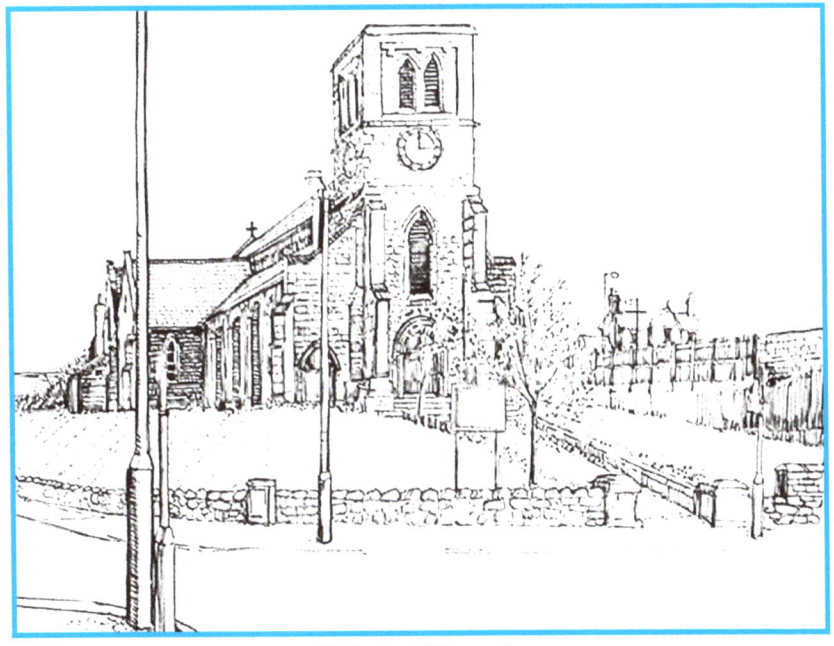

Trinity Church

35

In 1975 Mr Oliver, Deputy Editor of The Shields Gazette invited me to become "Art Critic". I'd always visited local exhibitions when I could, now there was an extra incentive. It was great to get a chance to publicise some of the artists I'd admired over the years from the Westoe, Harton, South Shields and Whitburn Art Clubs/Groups.

By this time I had introduced animation as a subject in class and the way the students responded blew me away. Pupils who formerly had little interesting in learning suddenly came alive. I have already covered the growth of my own animation and that of many others in my book/DVD "Animation a Handy Guide" if you're interested, if not, let's get back to views of Tyneside. Like this image of Marsden Bay painted on the spot in a howling gale.

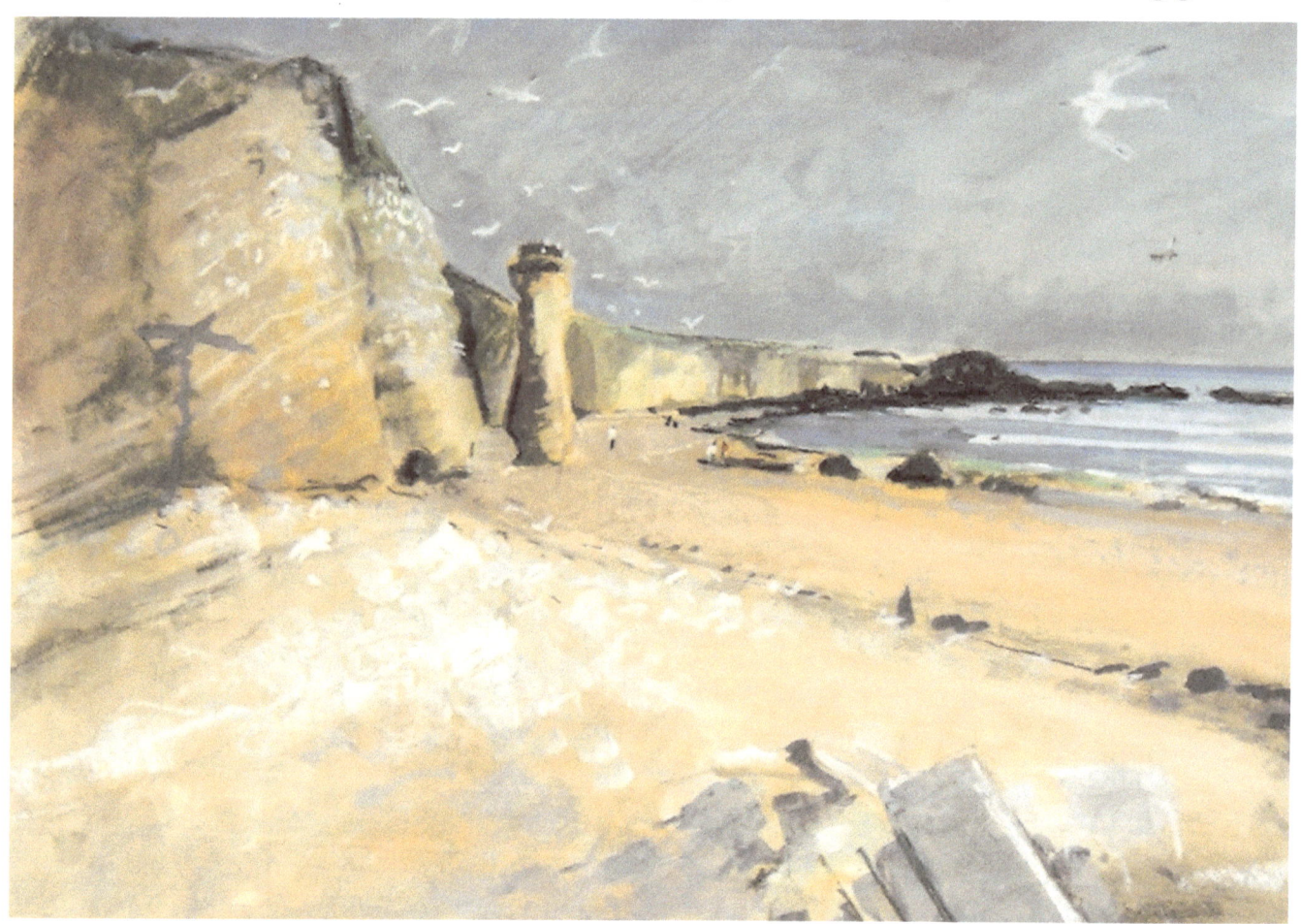

Marsden Bay 1978 acrylic and pastel

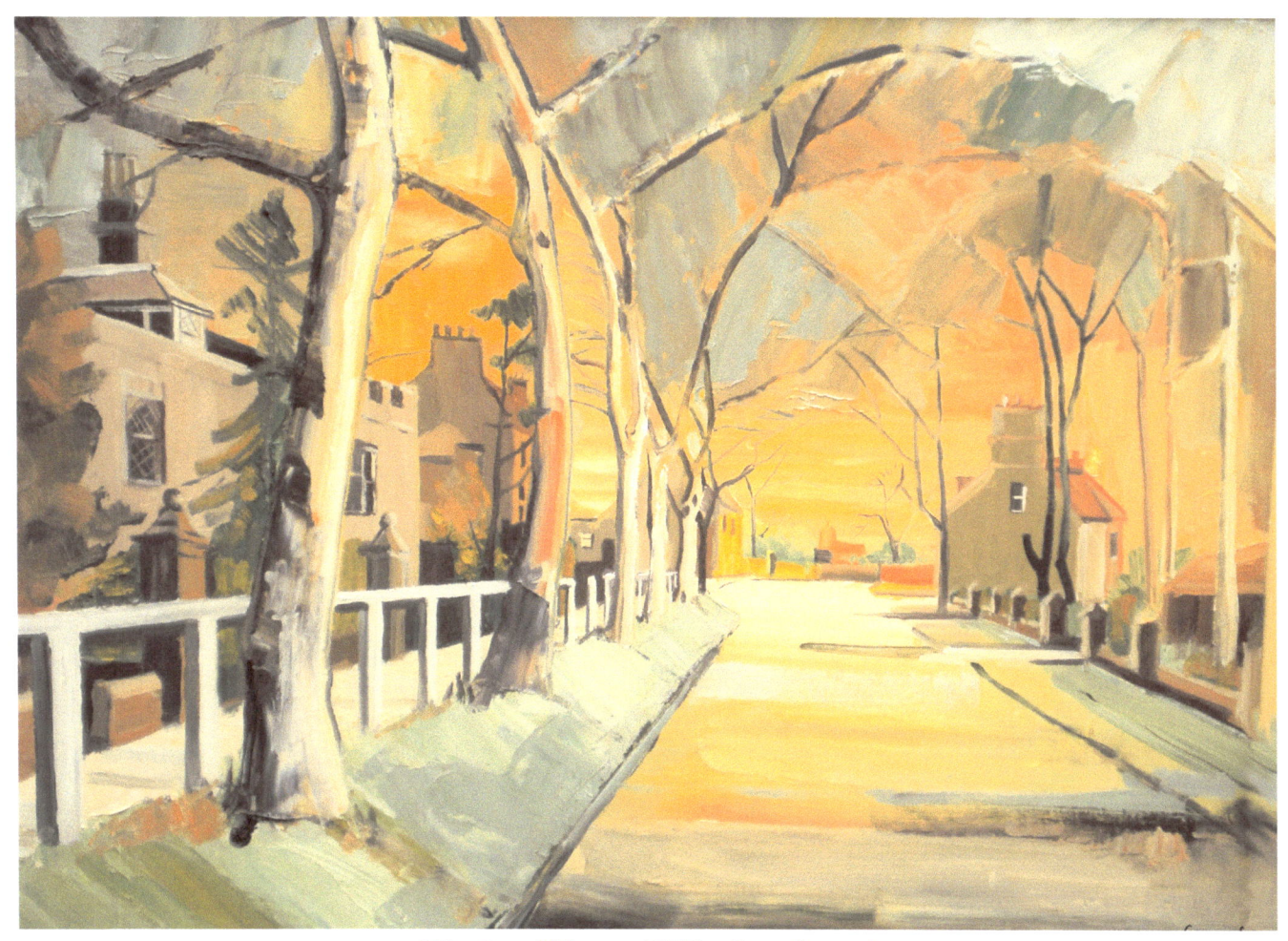

Westoe Village 1979 oil on board

Sylvia Welsh was my oldest friend from school, and Bridesmaid at my wedding.
As a thank you for this onerous duty I had promised her a painting of any subject she chose.
She picked Westoe Village and I eventually painted it for her fourteen years later.

Being an art critic meant I got to visit all the main galleries and their curators in the area from Vincent Rea at The Bede Gallery Jarrow, to Jean Rudkin at the Metal Art Precinct close by the river. Here I exhibited most of the pictures discussed over the past decade, alongside some excellent seascapes by Catherine Cookson and other "Women Artists of the North East.". The next year I held a second show there , this time it was cels and images from my films to celebrate the fact that I had moved into animation as a full time career.

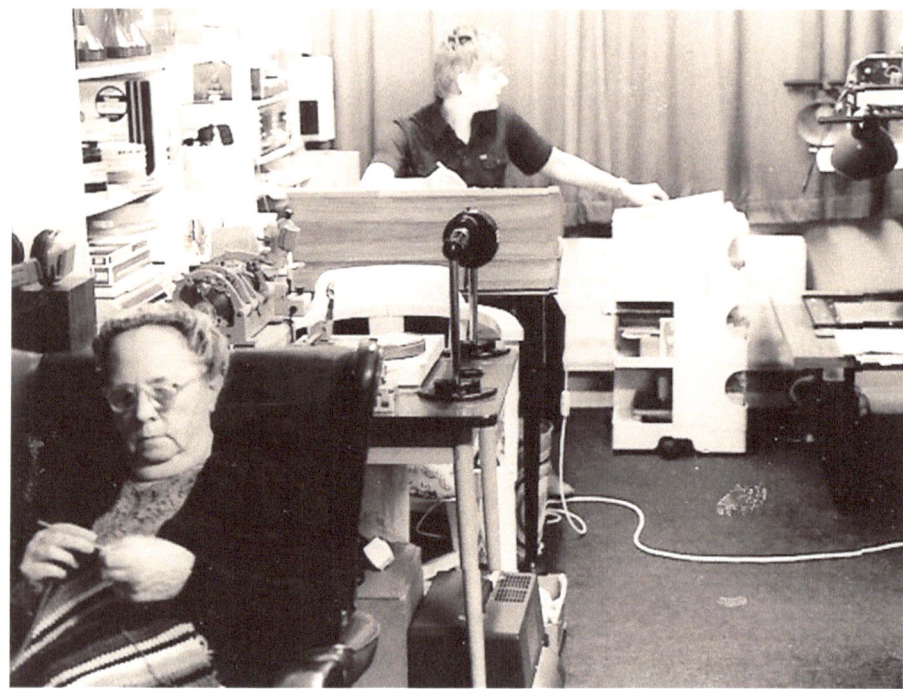

Work in Progress - Crotchet and Film - 1980

However I did not move very far. Just to my dining room at Meldon Avenue.

I'd always thought the only way to produce professional animation would be to have a large "Disney Like" studio with loads of dwarfs drawing, tracing, painting, and filming.

However I found it was possible to do it from my dining room table. As my Mam sat and crocheted stitch by stich making baby clothes for a local shop, I drew frame by frame to make movies to sell to world television.

'Everyone is an artist" and it does not matter whether you click a camera or crotchet hook you are creating something that helps to make life worthwhile.

As my Aunty Mabel said:-

"we all need something to pass the time"

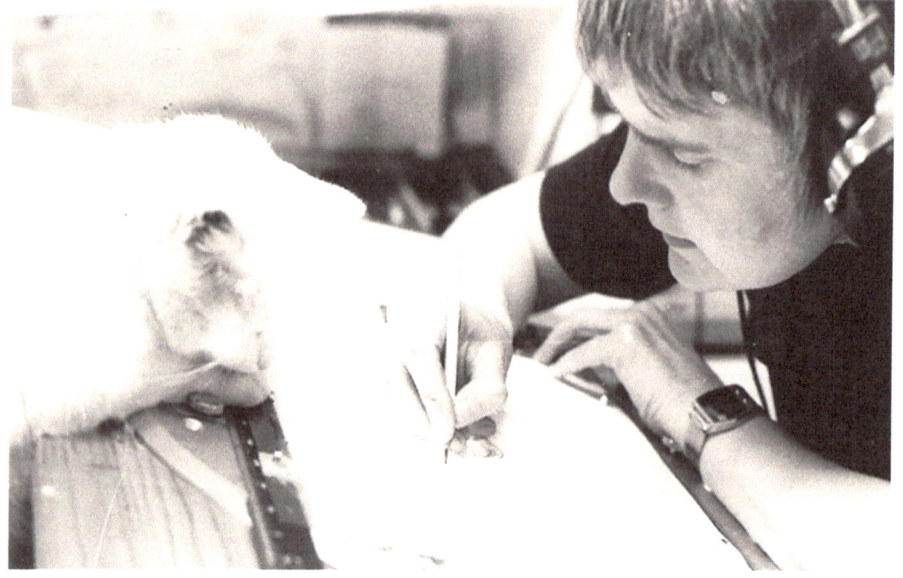

My View of Tyneside in 1980, animation and my cat Whitey

Nerys Johnson, an amazing artist in her own right, was Keeper-in-Charge at the Durham Light Infantry Museum and Arts Centre. I first got to know her when I ran animation workshops in her galleries, and over the years she became a family friend.

She offered me the opportunity for a large exhibition in 1985 where I could show paintings, drawings, art work from film and films. I think the cover sums that up! Inside she wrote an acknowledgement to all who had helped, including my Mother...

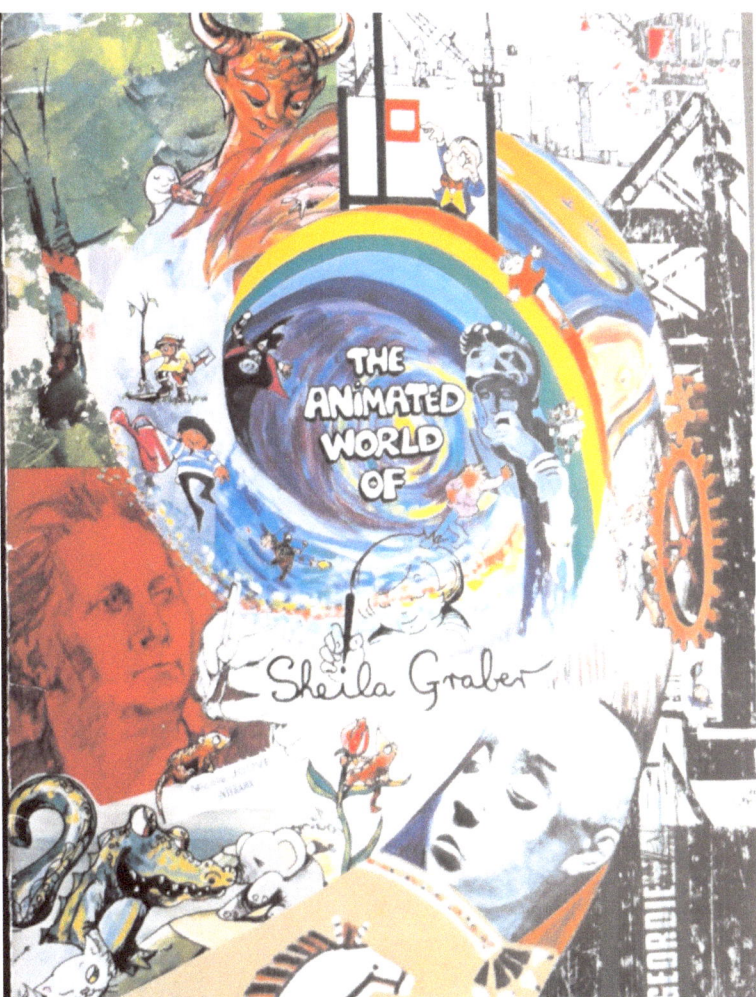

Cover of DLI Catalogue 1985

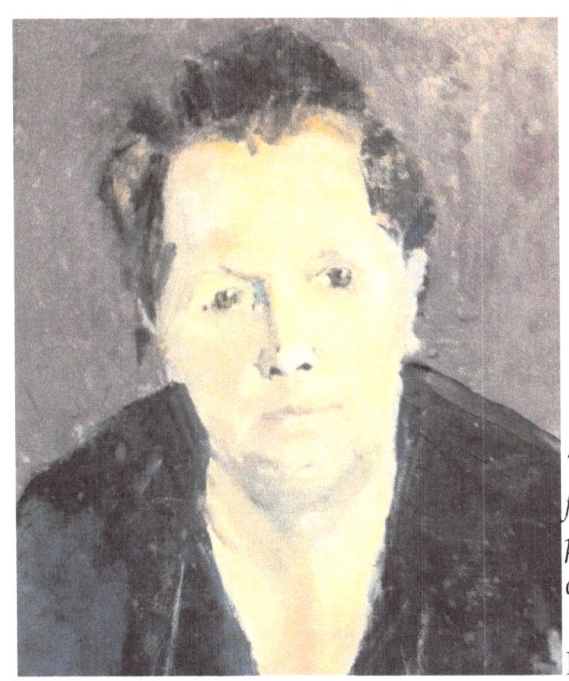

Portrait of the Artist's Mother
1957

"Finally, very special thanks to Sheila's "Ma", Mrs Graber, for putting up with so many disruptions, for the beautiful pieces of crotchet featured in the show, and for her quiet but constant support throughout the entire venture"

I agree with Nerys all the way, but if it were me writing it I'd alter the last phrase to *"My entire life"*.

Rod Hill was not only Chief Librarian at Shields Central Library but he was a true "Empresario" in the old Victorian Theatrical sense. The film theatre at the library thrived under his energies. Sporting a plush maroon jacket and bushy ginger beard he would introduce the fun packed evening with booming voice and genuine interest in his audience. The fact there was wine and loads of nibbles served by staff ,lead by Hildred Whale, who often"dressed up" to suit the occasion, helped a bit too!

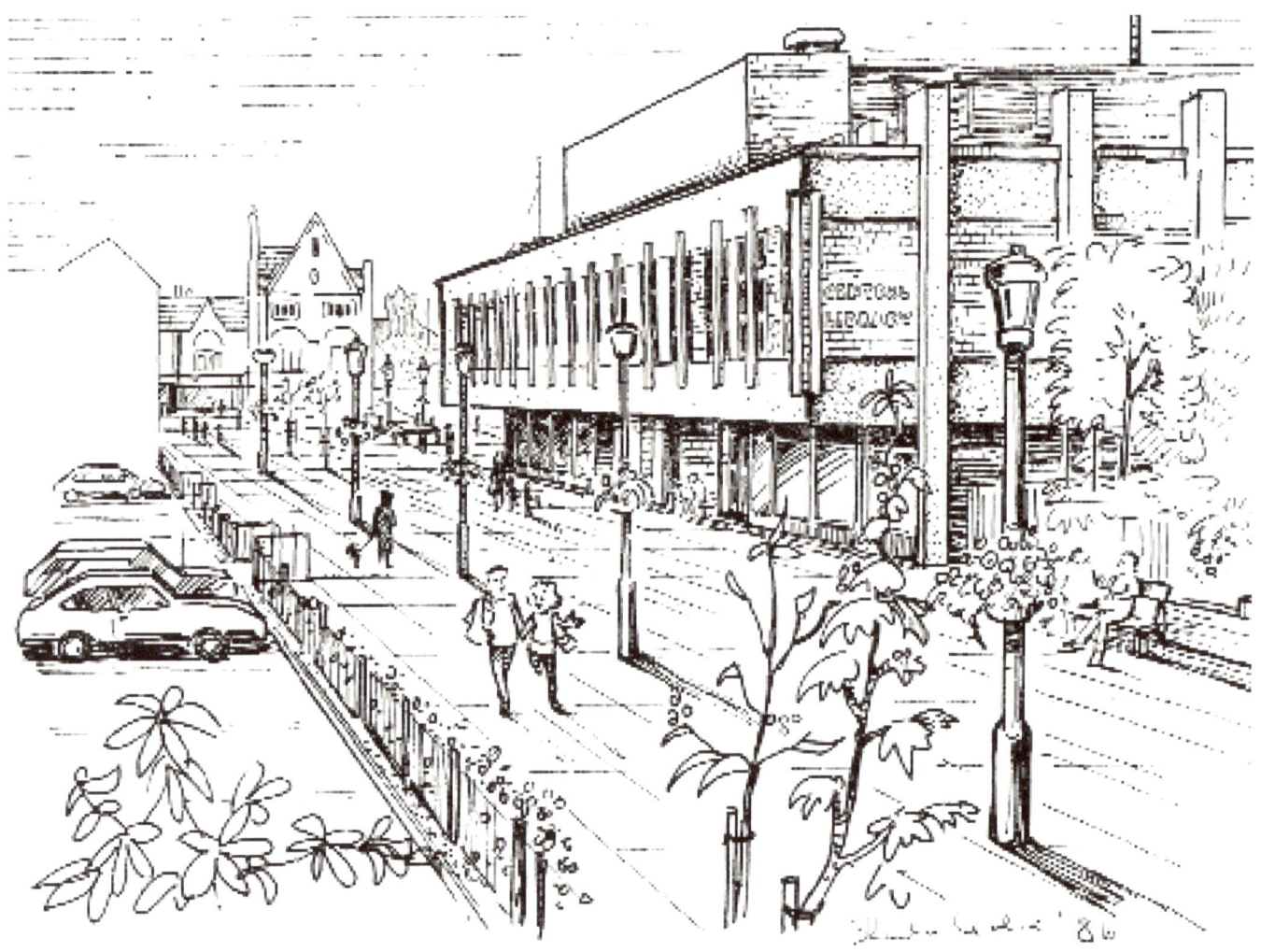

Central Library 1986

He kindly offered me a "Christmas Slot" where I could screen any films I wished. This was a great incentive to create material with not only a festive but local interest. So thanks to him I shot the film "My River Tyne". It was a history of the Tyne from Scots source to it's mouth at the Piers. Woven into it was a bit of my family history too. Rod always said I should make a movie/book called "Graber's Patch"I guess this is it! Below are four stills from the movie.

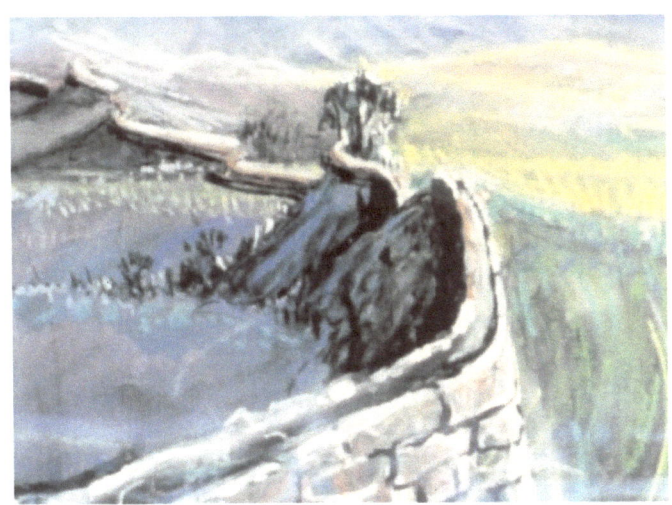

Hadrians Wall,pastel

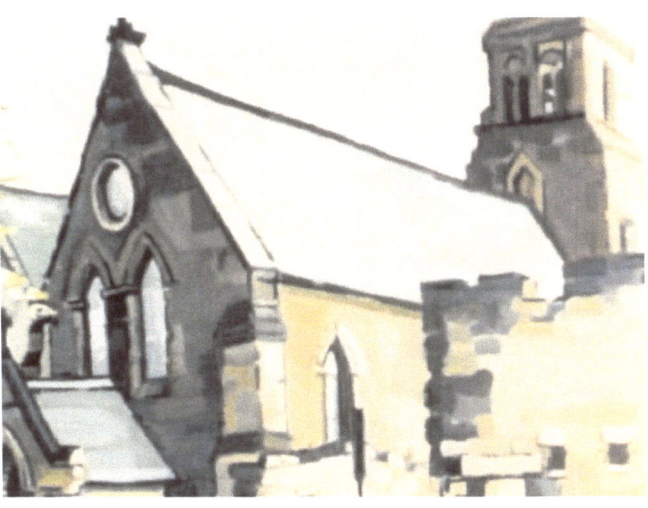

St Paul's Church Jarrow, oil painting

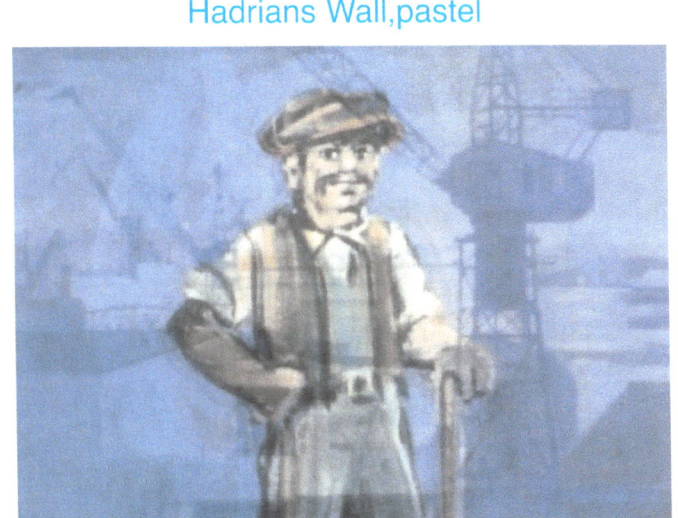

Ship Yard worker drawn in pastel, superimposed over the oil painting "Blue River Tyne"

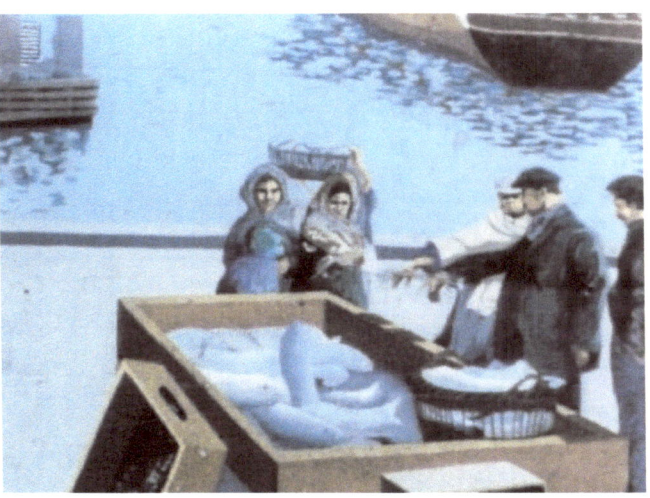

The Fish Quay, a small section of the brilliant mural designed by David Wilkinson along the wall of Commercial Road.

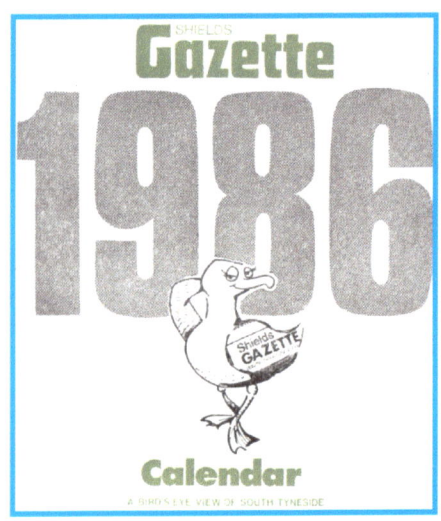

Mr Blackah editor at the Shields Gazette suggested I should make twelve images of Shields with a matching cartoon. "Splat" the Seagull was hatched.

**Try fitting the "Splats" below to the opposite scenes.
No prizes for getting them right!**

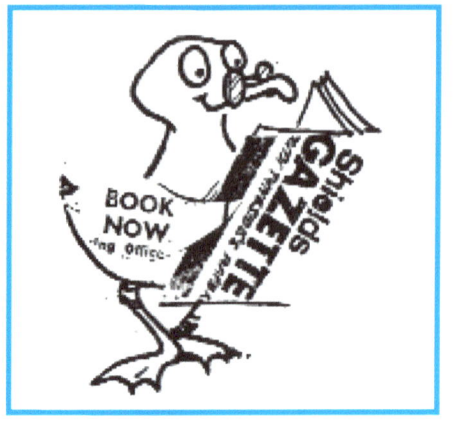

SPECTA-GULL
fits with previous "Library" page

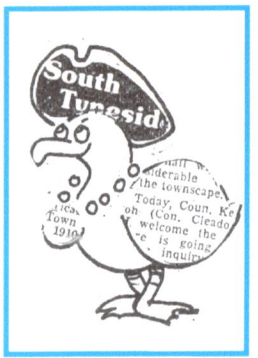

POLITI-GULL

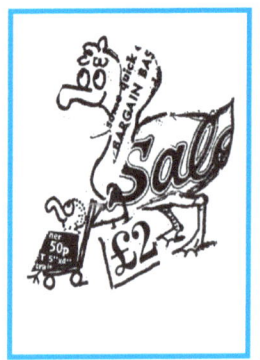

SALE-A-GULL

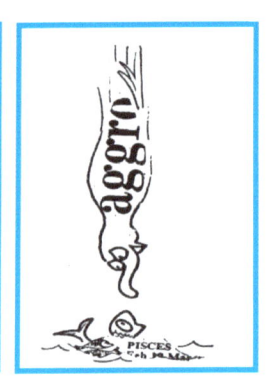

VERTI -GULL

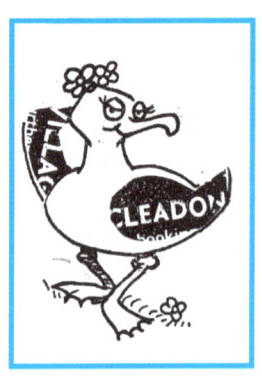

BEAUTI -GULL

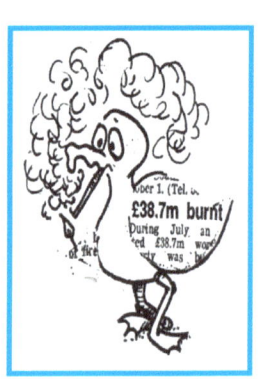

INFLAMMA-GULL

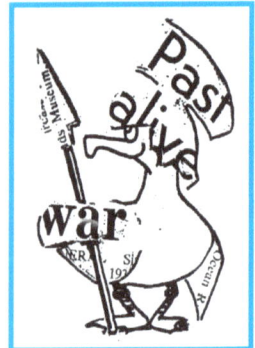
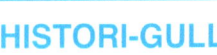

HISTORI-GULL

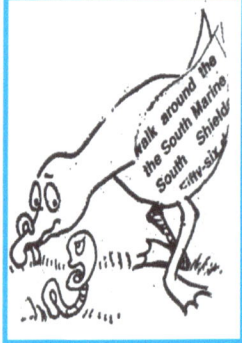

WRIG -GULL

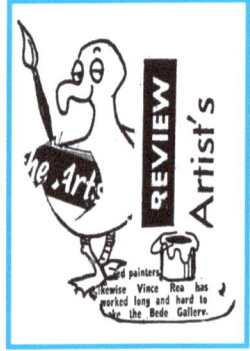

ARTY-GULL

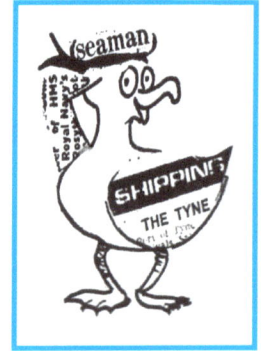

NAUTI-GULL

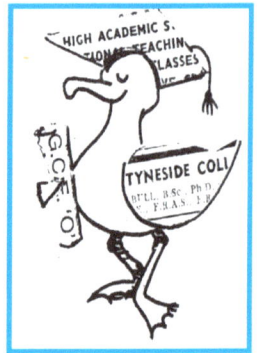

EDUCATION-GULL

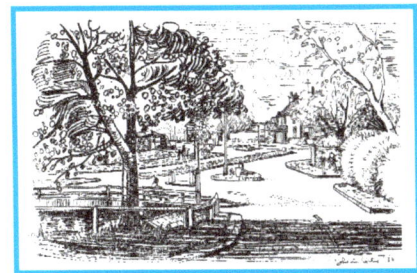

Cleadon Village

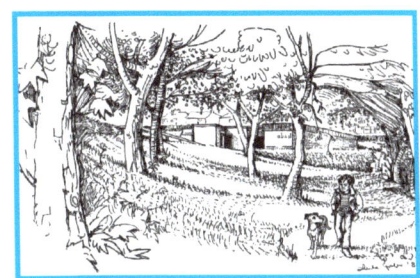

Bede Gallery Jarrow

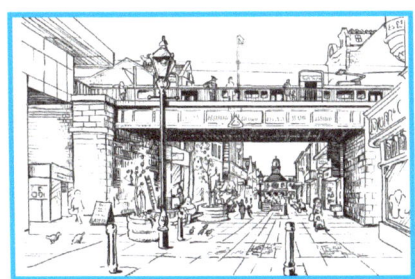

King Street

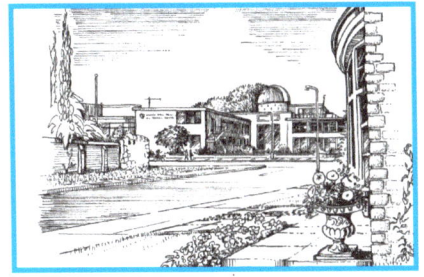

Marine & Technical College

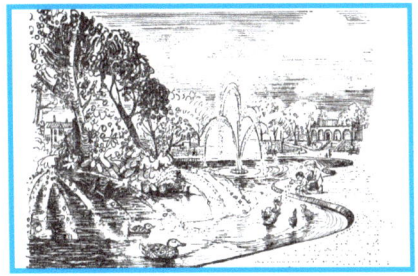

Marine Park

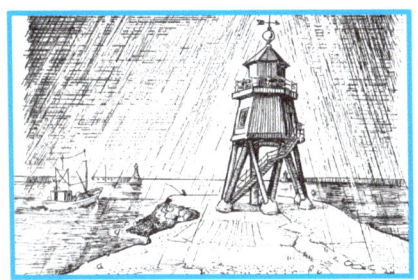

The Piers and Groyne

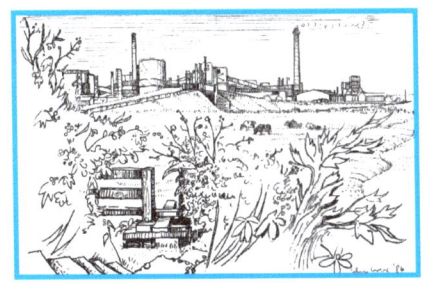

Monkton Coke Works

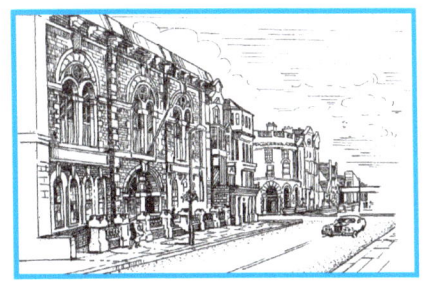

Museum Ocean Road

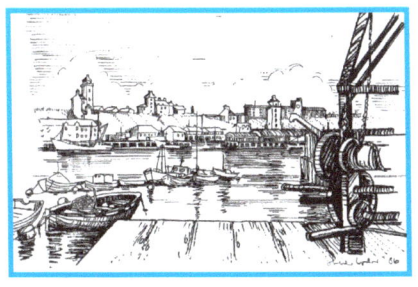

North Shields Fish quay

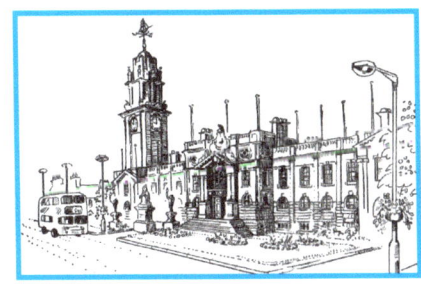

New Town Hall

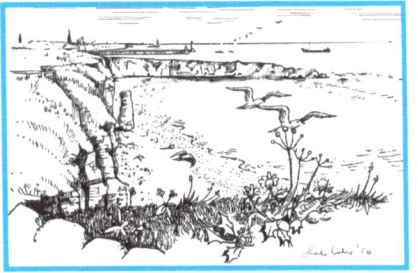

Marsden Bay

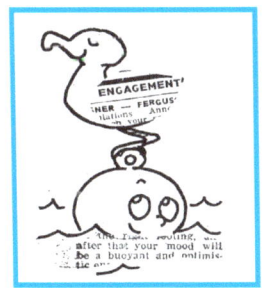

BOY MEETS-GULL

I must have drawn and painted my Mother sitting, knitting and crocheting hundreds of times. Over the years an image slowly grew in my head of her steadily crocheting a line that led us through the world and life itself...a "Lifeline" in fact.

"When I get the time" I thought I'll make that film starting from her finger in action.

So I began drawing the actual movement of her needle that would eventually be the opening action of the film...

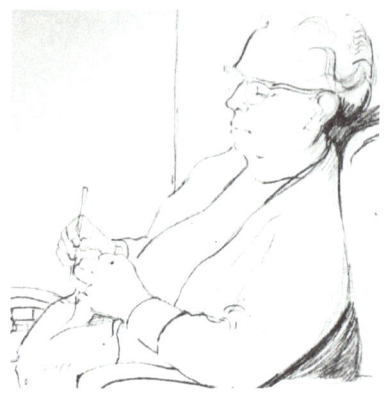

crocheting 1960

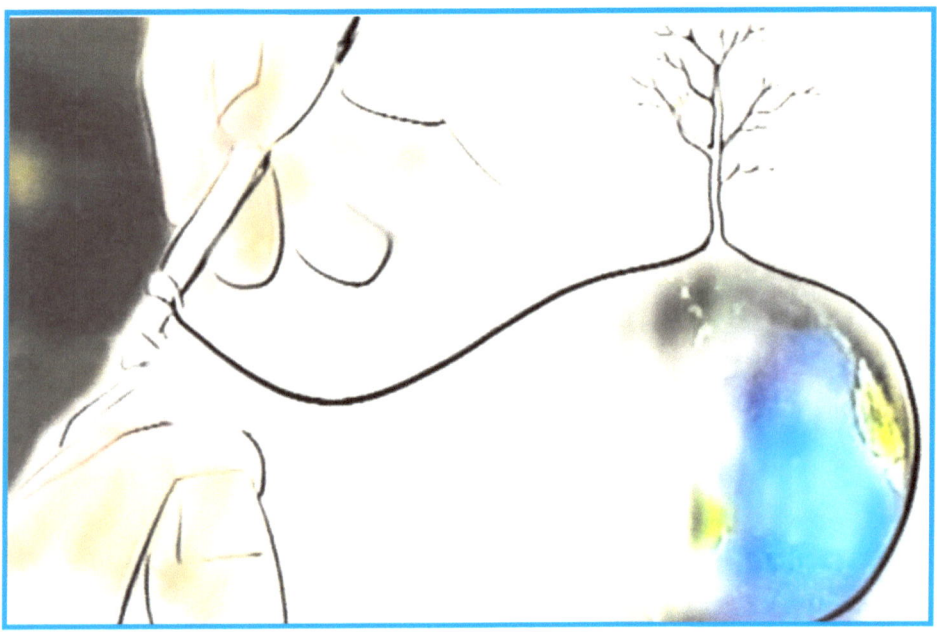

On 9.11.91 my Mam died in Mid-Crotchet. her last words were "Get on with your work".

Thanks to her following her Grandad Hunt the Herbalist's positive thinking philosophy she had not taken a pill or had a days illness in her life.

Finally succumbing to a massive heart attack at 89.

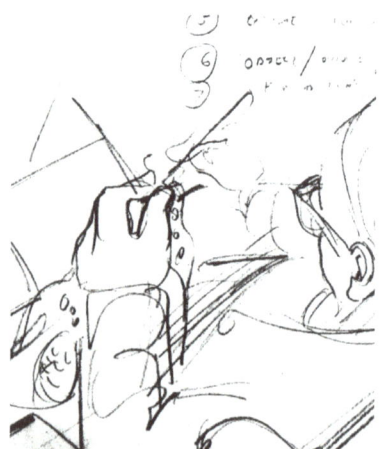

Analysis of hands in action1991

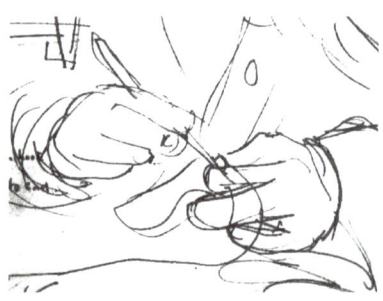

Following the line of the wool

44

I had no time or energy to continue with "Lifeline". Years later I was given the time thanks to Teeside University's "Animator in Residence Scheme". Whereby I was paid to teach and make my own film. In 2002 I completed it.

I was given the energy by Beethoven'e 'Ode to Joy" my soundtrack for the piece. I set out to use only places I knew in Tyneside and to follow what I had seen happening to those places, and me, in my lifetime.

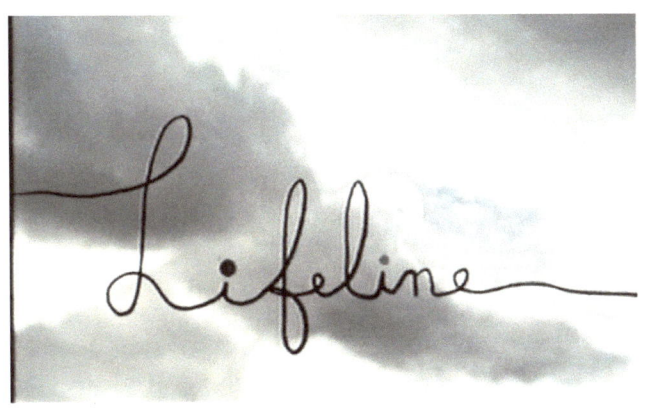

A line of wool writes the title

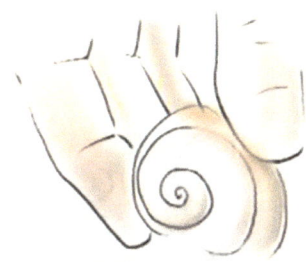

There used to be endless shells on our beaches, and shrimps in the pools.

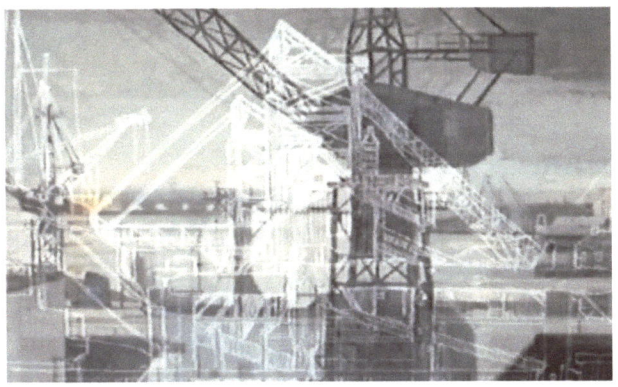

Pollution from industry killed most of the river and beach life.

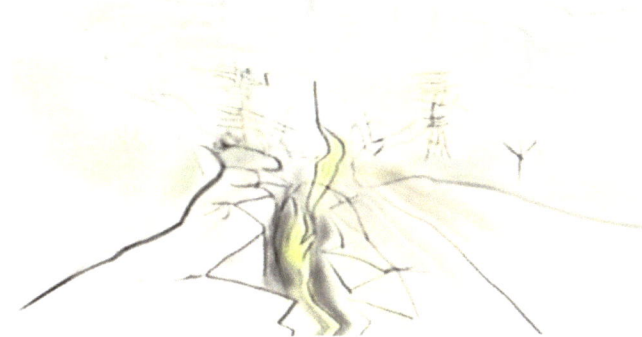

What if nature were allowed to take over again?

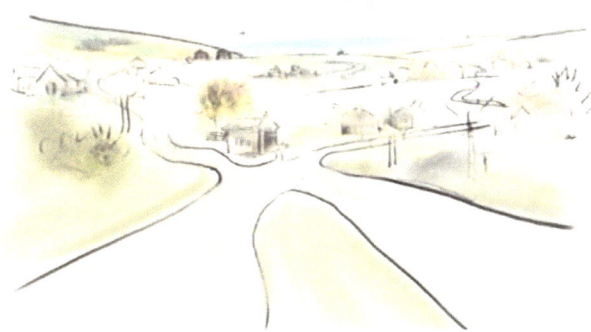

We might all have a cleaner, brighter, more meaningful life style.

45

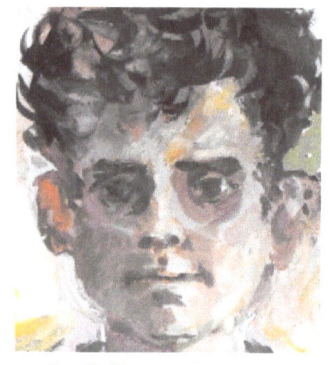

Self Portrait 1991

Shortly after my Mother's death I discovered I was adopted as a baby and had been born in Edinburgh. In seconds unanswered questions suddenly made sense. That's why I didn't look like anyone in the family, that's why I was often dressed in tartan and my folks took me every year to the Edinburgh Festival.That's why I never heard " you are good at art like your cousin, or "you have a wacky sense of humour like your brother." I feel that I got the best upbringing because I was adopted. I was an unknown quantity and having great parents they stood by me and encouraged, never imposed. I was allowed to be me.

Just wish I'd had the chance to tell them that they were the best.

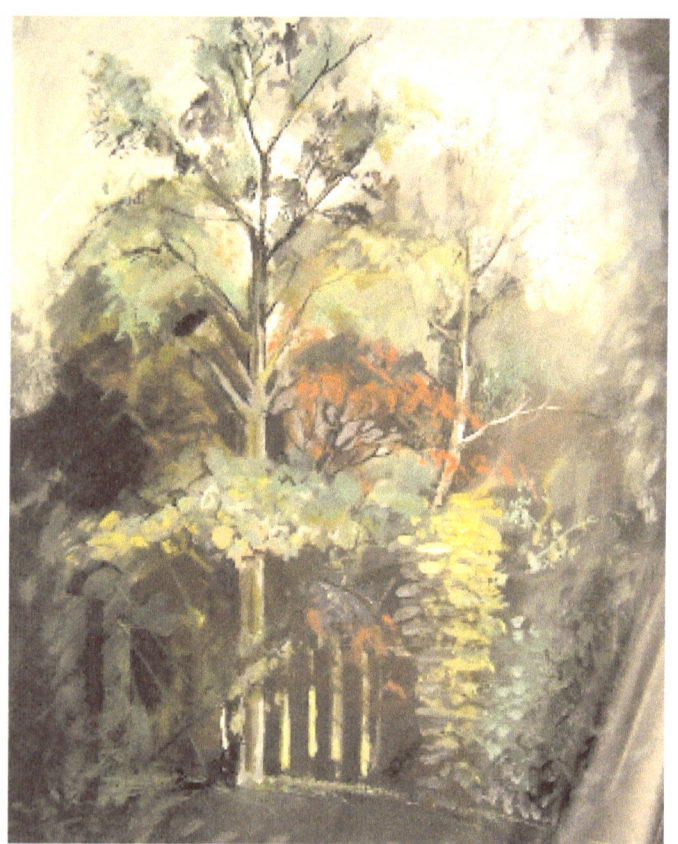

Dark Garden 1991

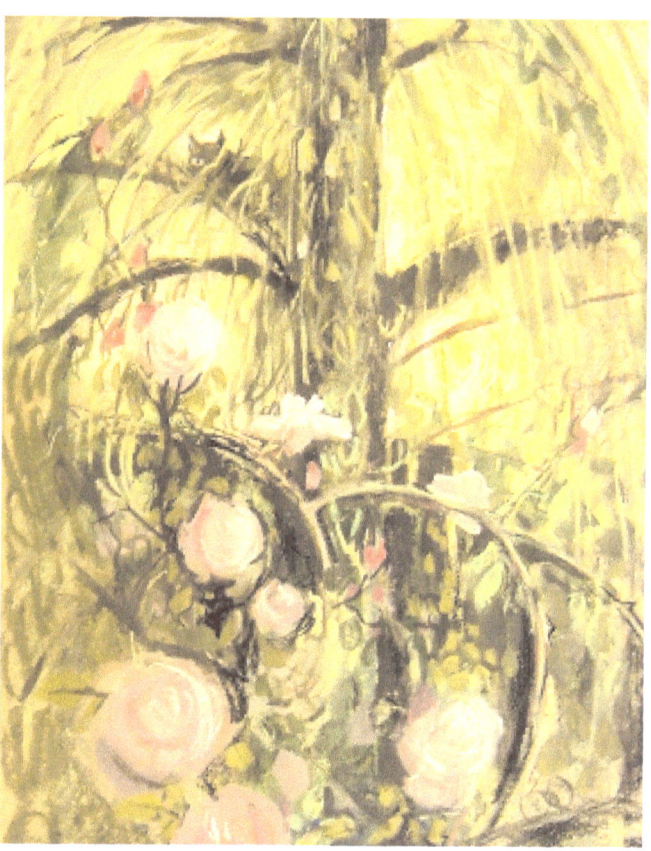

Garden with Roses and Cats 1993

Having spent much of my time at Meldon with my back to the window I started to look out and even went into the garden to paint..That was to be my Tyneside at that time.

You might have noticed a change of mood between the two gardens on the opposite page. To bring some life back into my home I collected twin kittens from a Hexham farm. Not being able to tell them apart I christened them Pixi and Dixi. If I drew the garden they came too. In fact they followed me round the block for walk.s. I guess in earlier times I'd have been burned as a witch. Wearing black, walking two cats out at night, into the idea of herbalism, even have a couple of moles on my face. I wouldn't have stood a chance.

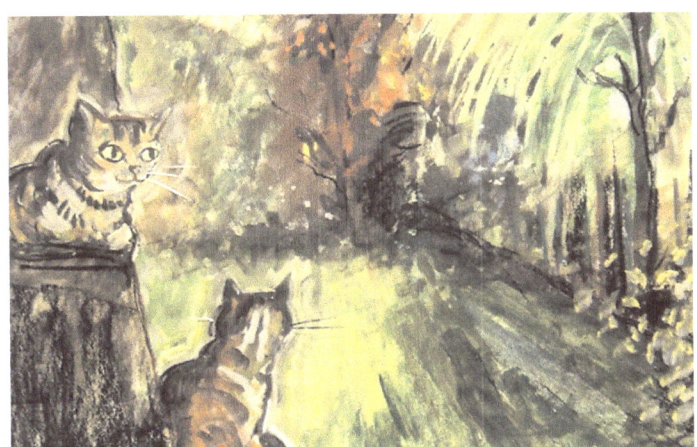

The Watchers

Quiet Evening

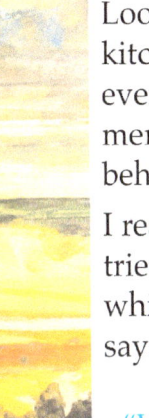

"We are all part of Nature" 1993

Looking through my kitchen window one evening my reflection merged into the trees behind, forming one image.

I reached for paints and tried to catch the moment, which reminded me of the saying by artist Paul Klee.

"We are all part of Nature within natural space."

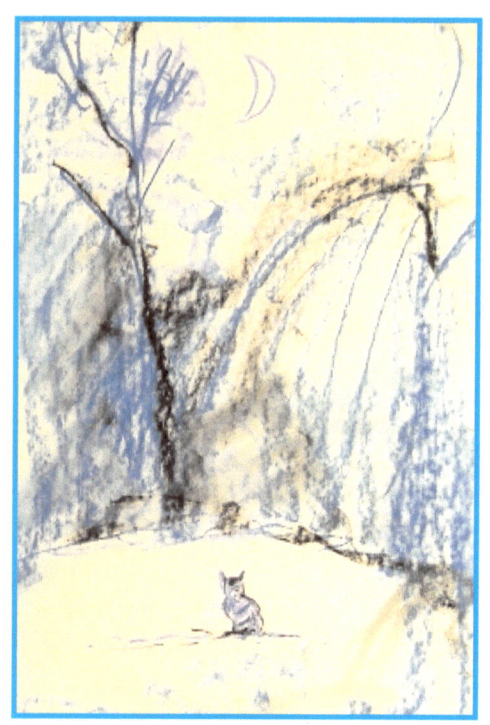

Dixi & Blue Moon 1994

By 1994 I had picked up momentum and work was flooding in again. Then Pixi, the leader of the twins, went missing. Dixi sat out all night in the middle of the lawn, My instinct told me Pixi was not coming back.

Hope sent me looking everywhere for the next fortnight.

No work was done until I discovered she had been run over in Temple Park Rd. I then woke up to the reality that I was way behind on a very large corporate/educational design job. The deadline was in two days, the only way I could meet that was to ask for help. I rang the talented artist (and poet)Scott Tyrrell who had spent some time with me the previous year on work experience.

 We met the deadline together and I employed him, By 1996 I had employed others both full and part-time and was running a busy Limited Company from home.

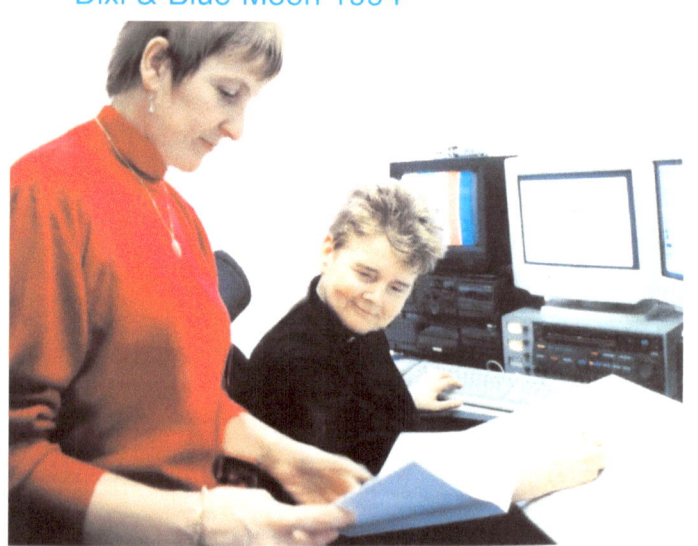

Myself and Jen at work 1996
Copyright Shields Gazette.

With the help of my Fellow Director Jen Miller it actually started to make a profit. A tiny echo of Walt, the animator and his brother Roy Disney, the business brain!

If you're an artist trying to make a living from your art, find an honest and reliable business manager to work with you .

It's virtually impossible to put a realistic monetary value on your own work.

It is extremely rare when you actually get paid for what you love to do. It had happened with "Lifeline" and now it happened again!

Ray Spencer, Director of the Custom's House and his team knew my work and my love of the River so it was suggested that I take part in an International project "Cargo" .
My part was to run animation workshops with Port of Tyne Personnel and make an animated film about "Cargo on the River ". Below are 6 stills from the final animated movie "Tyne Cargo". It covers the history of our river from Dug Out Canoe to Container ships.

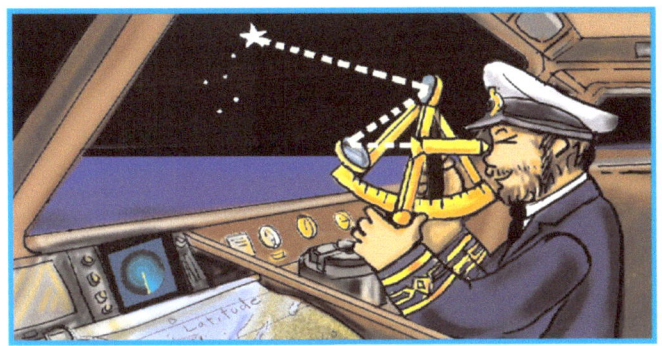
Navigating by the stars on tankers .

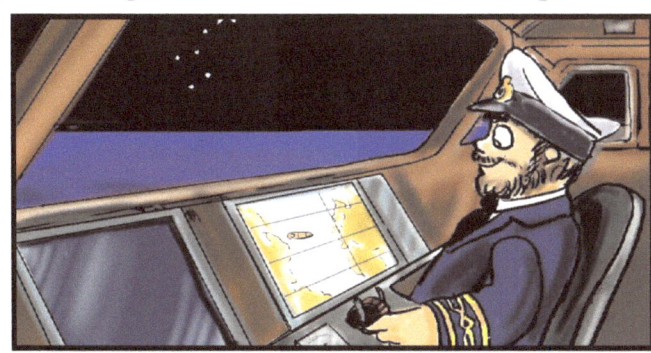
Satellite Navigation on Container Ships.

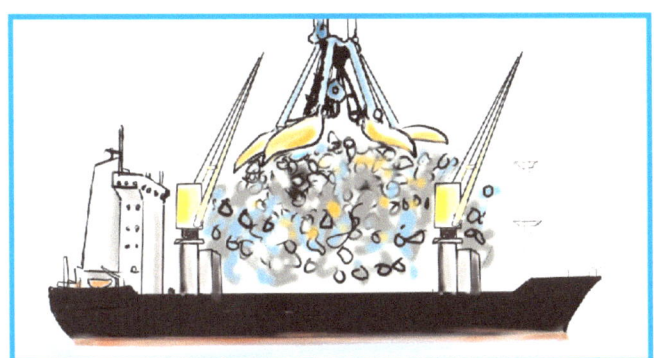
Scrap metal exported out from Port of Tyne.

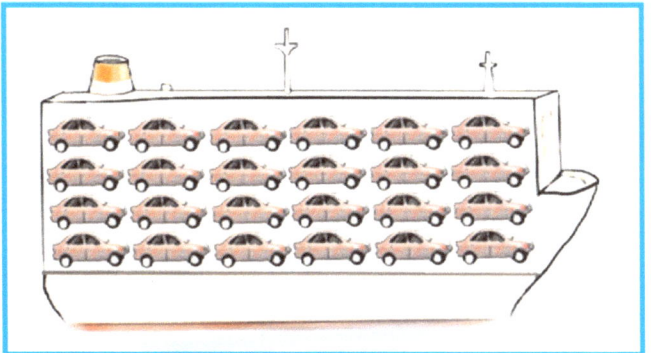
Imported back as cars.

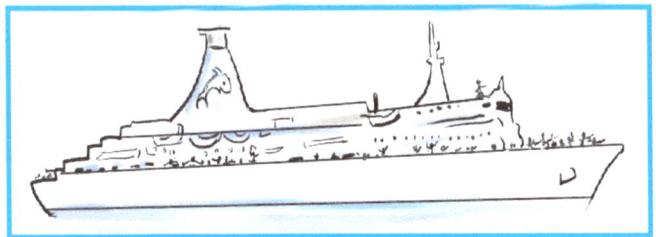
Ferry to Europe with people as cargo.

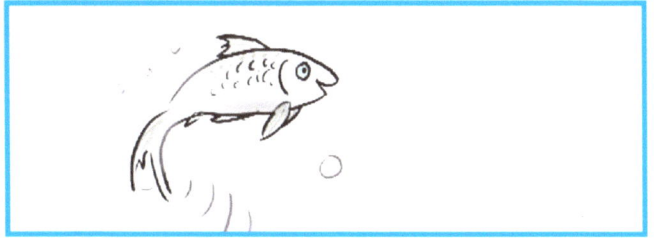
Salmon can now live in our cleaner Tyne.

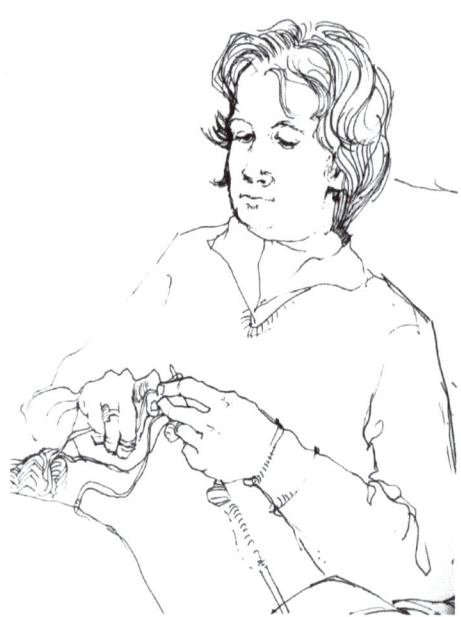

Sylvia Welsh, my oldest friend sadly died suddenly and far too soon. She was a great patron of "Save the Children" and in her retirement she had plans for lots more charity ventures to support them. Unfortunately, they were not to be.

In early 2003 my colleague Jen said "Would I ever retire and make the movies and books I'd always planned."
I thought... "well no, not if I stay here, there is far too much work to be done." That was the first glimmer of the idea that we would actually move from Tyneside.

Sylvia knittiing blanket squares
for "Save the Children"
1962

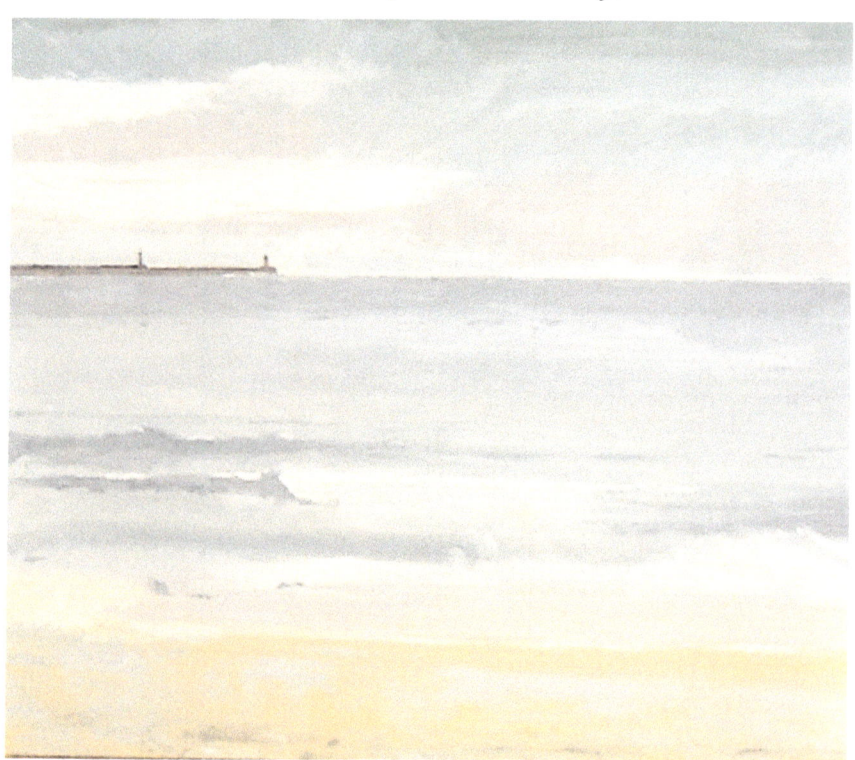

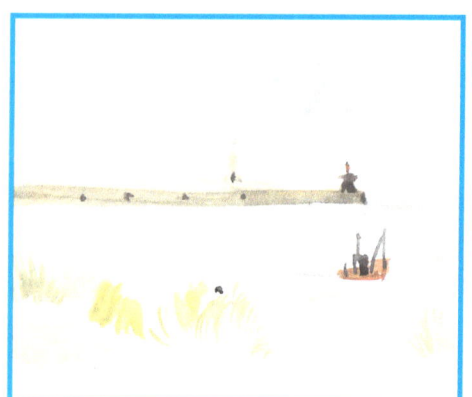

Water colour sketch and final oil painting for "Two Piers" Shields Harbour 2004

The final decision came in late 2003 . We then booked in for a "Goodbye Retrospective" exhibition at the Customs House in 2004. " The World of Sheila Graber"..

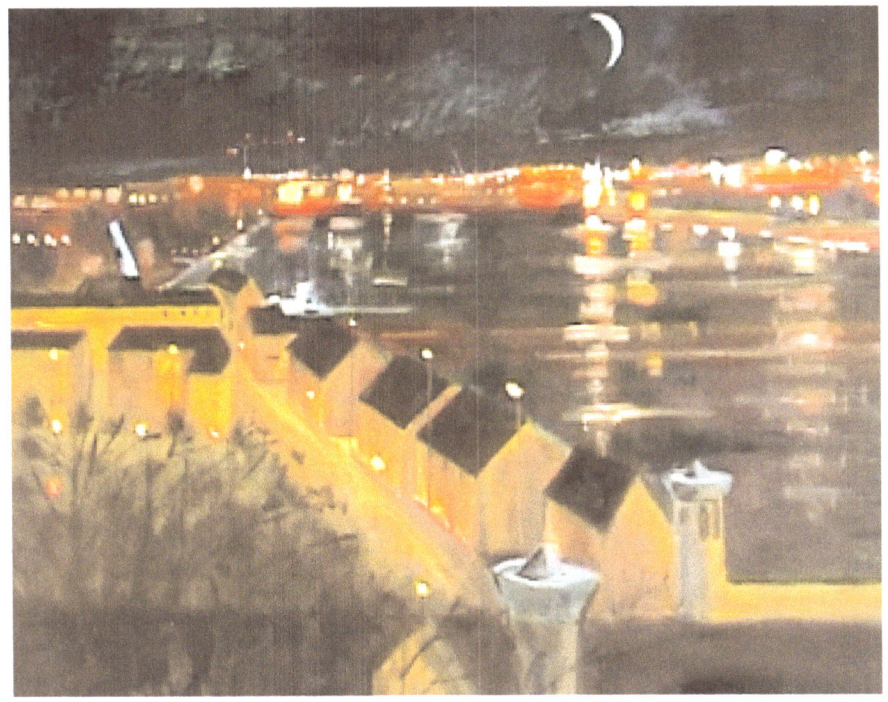

For the first time I saw hanging in one place a range of work I'd created over 50 years. Looking back I reckon that show gave me the idea of creating this book..

So a huge thanks to the Customs House for displaying the show, to John Lightfoot for opening it

...but most of all to YOU for travelling on this personal journey with me.

I hope it has triggered many memories of your own of "Canny Shields."

Tyne at Night, overlooking the illuminated Ferry Landing just visible to the left. 2004

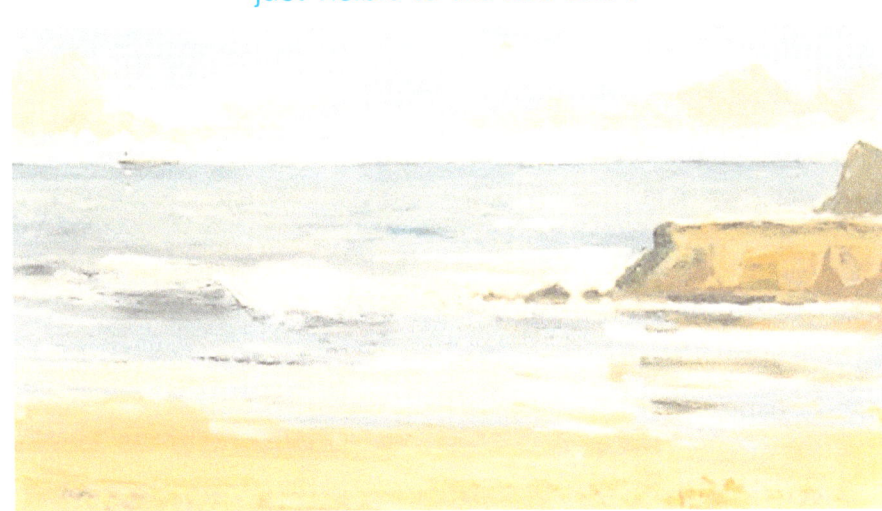

Trow Rocks 2004

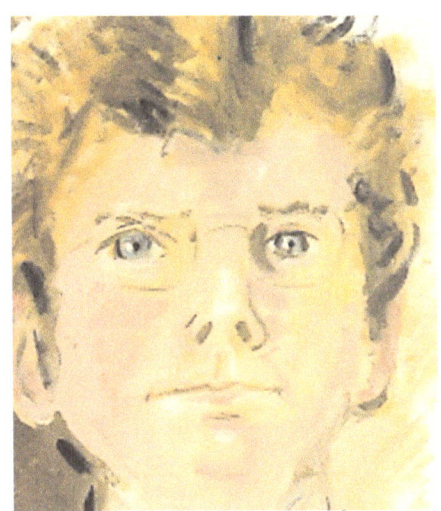

Self Portrait 2004

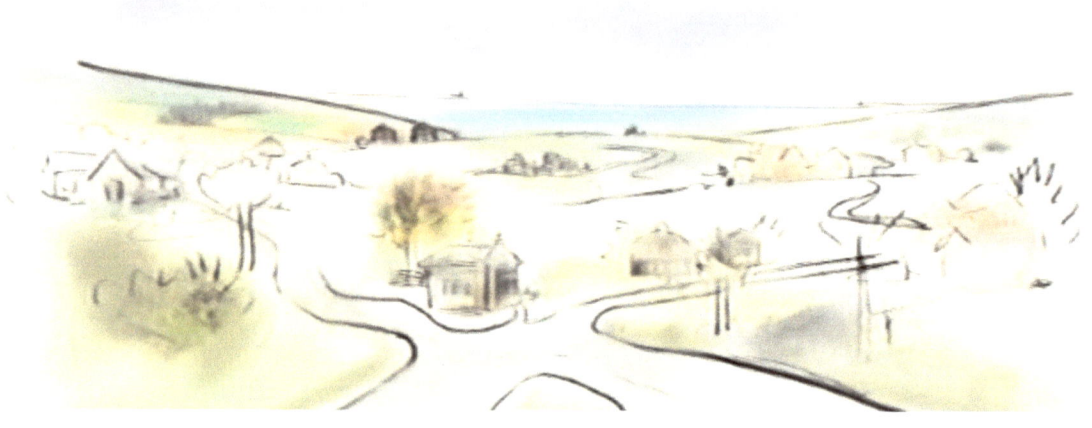

Final Image from "Lifeline" 2002

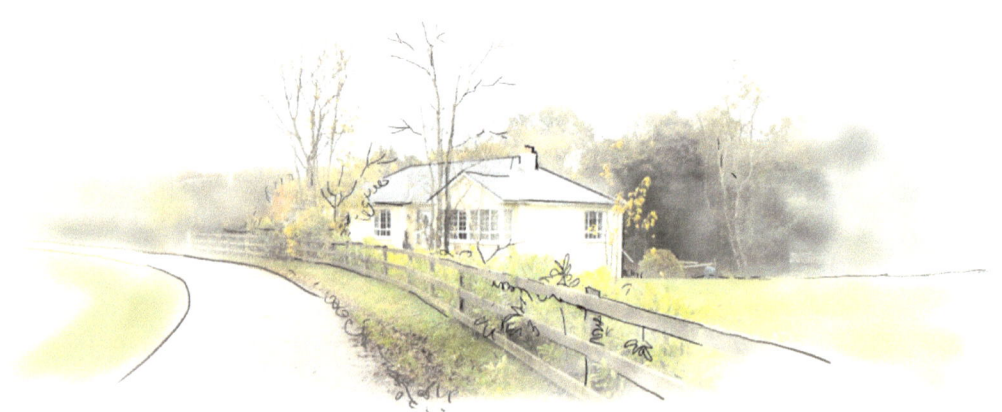

Our "Sandancer" home in Ireland 2005

The last image from"Lifeline" was created from my imagination in 2002.
When I made that film I had no wish at all to move from Shields.
Now we live in a house (called Sandancer) in the country, not far from the sea,
just like in the film !

As Walt Disney said

"If you can dream it you can do it"

See all movies mentioned in the book, lots more images of Tyneside
and even other places in the world !
On our website
www.graber-miller.com

THANKS

I would like to thank **everyone who ever taught me** and **everyone I ever taught** in Tyneside
for helping to extend my horizons.

Huge thanks to **Hildred Whale, John Lightfoot, Janis Blower and Ray Spencer** for so kindly
taking the time to write their views of Tyneside.
Their memories really bring the book alive and give it universal meaning.

Finally thanks to **Jen Miller** for encouraging me to sort through hundreds of bits of paper,
and thousands of words to help create this book.

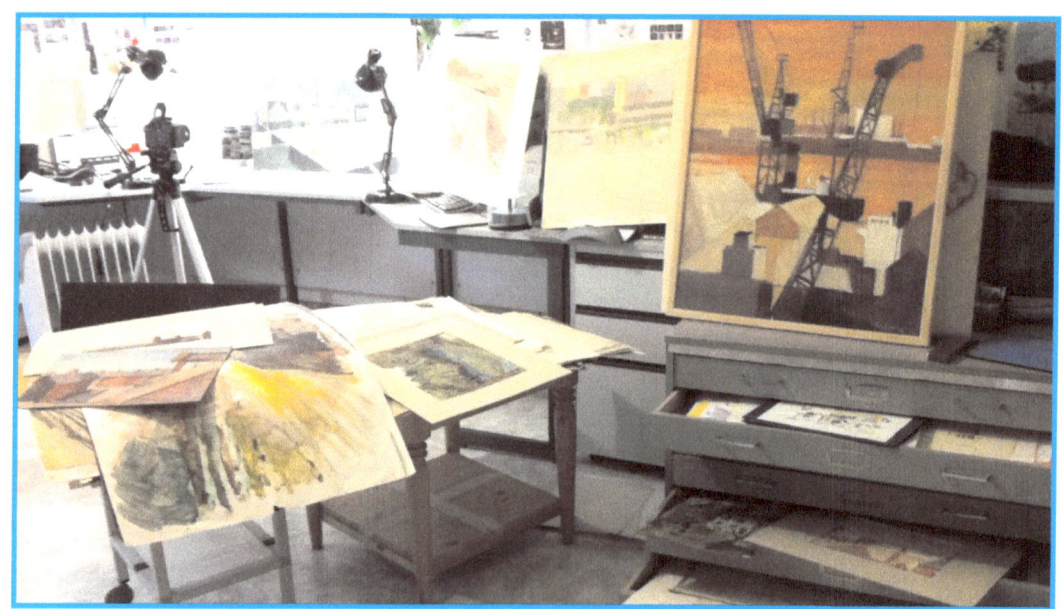

Sorting in progress...

Copyright/Credits for Imagesand stills from Movies

LIFELINE - Page 44/45

University of Teesside, Middlesbrough Arts Development, Northern Arts,
Northern Cultural Skills Partnership.

TYNE CARGO Page 49

Helix Arts & Customs House South Shields,
Project Funder- Northern Rock

www.ingramcontent.com/pod-product-compliance
Lightning Source LLC
Chambersburg PA
CBHW051053180526
45172CB00002B/625